World of Art

Kathleen Raine (1908–2003), poet and critic, was educated at Girton College, Cambridge. She loved Blake throughout her long and distinguished literary career, and her A. W. Mellon Lectures in Washington, DC, in 1962, which became the basis of her two-volume study *Blake and Tradition* (1968), played a vital part in establishing that Blake, previously known mainly as a self-taught eccentric, belongs to a long and coherent tradition of Platonic, Hermetic and mystical thought. She wrote a number of books of poetry, and her *Collected Poems* appeared in 2000. Her other books included *From Blake to a Vision* (1979), *Blake and the New Age* (1979), *The Human Face of God: William Blake and the Book of Job* (Thames & Hudson, 1982) and four volumes of autobiography.

Colin Trodd is Senior Lecturer in the School of Arts, Languages and Cultures at the University of Manchester. He has published extensively on Romantic painting an the art institutions of the Victorian and Edwardian eras, including *Visions of Blake: William Blake in the Art World 1830–1930* (2012), the first full-length examination of Blake's artistic afterlife.

1 *When the Morning Stars Sang Together, c.* 1804–7. One of the watercolour drawings made for Thomas Butts.

World of Art

William Blake
Kathleen Raine

New edition
With a preface by Colin Trodd

To Kerrison Preston, honoured
friend and interpreter to all who
come to learn from Blake

First published in 1970 in the United Kingdom
by Thames & Hudson Ltd, 181A High Holborn,
London WC1V 7QX

www.thamesandhudson.com

First published in 1970 in the United States
of America by Thames & Hudson Inc.,
500 Fifth Avenue, New York, New York 10110

www.thamesandhudsonusa.com

This new edition 2021

William Blake © 1970, 2019 and 2021
Thames & Hudson Ltd, London

Text by Kathleen Raine

Preface and Select Bibliography by Colin Trodd

Art direction and series design: Kummer & Herrman
Layout: Kummer & Herrman

British Library Cataloguing-in-Publication Data
A catalogue record for this book is available from
the British Library

Library of Congress Control Number 2020933630

ISBN 978-0-500-20472-6

Printed and bound in China through
Asia Pacific Offset Ltd

Contents

Preface to the New Edition

Kathleen Raine's *William Blake* was first published by
Thames & Hudson in their celebrated 'World of Art' series
in 1970. This series broke new ground in different ways:
production values were far beyond comparable publications
in this modest price bracket; each volume was designed with
real panache; and the physical pleasure of holding, handling
and reading the books was greatly enhanced by the excellent
alignment of image and text. As can be appreciated, this
attention to the visual features and details of the art book
would be of great benefit to a volume on William Blake,
the master of the creative integration of poetry, imagery
and decoration.

Before proceeding any further, it is necessary to say a few
words about Raine's life. She was born in Ilford, Essex, in
1908 and died in 2003. She studied natural sciences at Girton
College, Cambridge, and graduated in 1929. Her university
contemporaries included Anthony Blunt and Jacob Bronowski,
both of whom would go on to produce brilliant books on Blake
during glittering careers as public intellectuals. Raine married
Hugh Sykes Davies, a poet, novelist and academic, in 1930. The
pair moved in avant-garde circles: Davies was a co-organizer of
the legendary London International Surrealist Exhibition (1936);
Raine became friends with the poet David Gascoyne, the film-
maker Humphrey Jennings and the art theorist Herbert Read,
three of the most talented members of the English Surrealist
Group. Like many literary figures of her generation, she was
brought into contact with left-wing ideas, first as a student and
then through her involvement in Mass Observation, a social
research project established in 1937 and directed and organized
by her second husband, the poet, journalist and sociologist
Charles Madge. By the early 1940s, however, she had rejected

radical politics and social engagement in favour of the study of systems of spirituality, myth and magic, a mentality shared by a new circle of friends including the novelist Gay Taylor, the painter Winifred Nicholson and the poet-painter David Jones. *Stone and Flower*, Raine's first volume of poetry, accompanied by designs by Barbara Hepworth, was published in 1943. The neo-romantic sensibility proposed in these poems, where human time offers a set of glimpses into sacred patterns and universal states, remained intact for the rest of Raine's life. She co-founded *Temenos*, a periodical, in 1981 and the Temenos Academy in 1990, both of which promoted the idea that art was expressive of the sacred belief-systems of East and West. In three highly unconventional autobiographical volumes – *Farewell Happy Fields* (1974), *The Land Unknown* (1975) and *The Lion's Mouth* (1977) – Raine set out to produce a history of the development of her visionary awakening into a condition of timeless life beyond individual personality. It is worth pointing out that this vision of life as spiritual growth was derived from W. B. Yeats' model of the gyre, the order of development that explained the intersection of individual life and the collective living mind in different historical periods. Yeats, in turn, thought that Blake's art and poetry could be described as invocations or spells, attempts to summon the magical powers working within a gyre. Yeats' *A Vision* (1925 and 1937), which outlines his gyre theory, is called 'extraordinary' in Raine's *William Blake*.

We should note from the outset that Raine's vision of Blake was controversial, as it went against the grain of post-war Anglo-American scholarship, where Blake's art was identified with late eighteenth-century revolutionary iconoclasm, or with the development of a personalized mythological scheme derived from apocalyptic, but socially radical, Protestantism. In both cases, it was conjectured, Blake's temperament drew from forms of popular or common culture; as artist, poet and thinker Blake was a social reformer or revolutionary, a timely prophet against what would be called the world of dehumanization or alienation.

Raine's Blake was in complete opposition to these well-entrenched schools of thought, which were supported by numerous influential figures including Jacob Bronowski (*William Blake: The Man without a Mask*, 1943), David V. Erdman (*Blake: Prophet Against Empire*, 1954), E. P. Thompson (*The Making of the English Working Class*, 1963) and Theodore Roszak (*The Making of a Counter Culture*, 1969). Each of these authors presented Blake as a peerless exemplar of social criticism, a forerunner of Karl Marx in his hostility to industrialism and capitalism. *Blake and Tradition* (1968), Raine's best-known and most detailed reading of Blake as artist, thinker and poet, rejects this body of thought. The central thesis of her two-volume, eight-hundred-page epic, based on a set of lectures given in the early 1960s, is easy enough to outline. Blake's art, she claims, worked from, and was enriched by, traditional myths and symbols. This attitude to art-making remained unaltered throughout Blake's long career. It was a system of universal wisdom, something devised to allow viewers to engage with the symbiotic logic at work in his paintings, prints and poetry. After the early 1790s, he remained aloof from the world of revolutionary politics.

Matters become more complex when attention turns to the critical arc of Raine's argument. *Blake and Tradition* connects Blake to alchemy, Jewish mysticism and classical mythology. It compares Blake's poems and images to Orphic, Neoplatonic, Gnostic and Hermetic sources. The purpose of all this is to indicate that Blake's mythology constitutes the integration of different examples of mysticism and magic. Raine calls this composite tradition the Perennial Philosophy, a process of cultural renewal where different strands of belief cohered around a central theme and value: that bodily life is a descent into the world of time and space, the exile of the soul from eternal life. Hence, Jewish, Orphic, Neoplatonic, Mithraic, Gnostic and Hermetic writings and symbols offer slightly different aspects of a single spiritual truth. It was this composite tradition that Blake strove to picture in his complex, many-sided symbolic forms. Here Raine was in broad agreement with a small group of earlier writers on Blake, such as W. B. Yeats, Denis Saurat and Désirée Hirst, all of whom presented him as a religious rebel with access to an underground tradition of metaphysical thought.

There are tensions within this model. An important part of Raine's argument was that Blake should not be called an activist artist: he was not interested in translating his inner feelings into social art. Her Blake belonged to the world of imagination, but this imagination was universal, not personal. Put differently, Raine believed that Blake's art was designed to address an audience by using a pre-existing public language, albeit one marginalized by what she saw as the arid formalism of eighteenth-century British culture. Nevertheless, Raine's version of an audience, one which is equipped with an extraordinary ability to engage with and assimilate a bewildering range of sources, cultures and traditions, is impossible to reconcile with the reality of eighteenth-century reading communities. In this respect, it might be best to

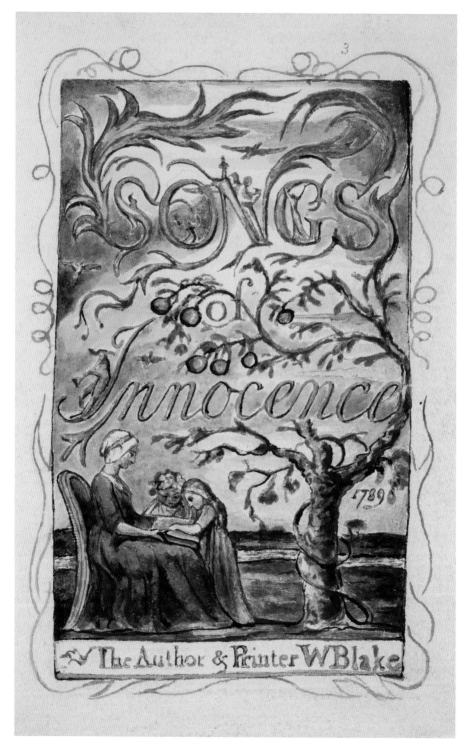

characterize Raine's position as a fantasy of purity, a condition where a wondrously erudite author claims special access to the cultural authority and esoteric wisdom he or she imagines to be present in the subject under review.

Blake and Tradition was written for scholars and researchers interested in a multitude of cultural matters; *William Blake* was aimed at a general readership. In seeking to understand the distinctiveness and value of Raine's second book, we must begin by noting that it too offers a systematic analysis of Blake's art and thought. Raine's account of Blake's designs and poems is vivid, lucid, zestful and unencumbered by the abstract terminology favoured by many academic writers. In what follows, I want to highlight her clear-sighted ability to get to grips with some of the fundamental features of Blake's sparkling imagery.

The thread that runs through *William Blake* is Raine's effort to engage with the fierce exuberance of Blake's art, as well as its capacity to picture a world that seems to 'possess a reality, a coherence, a climate and an atmosphere of its own'. She stresses the peculiar internal dynamic of Blake's artistic imagination, a mentality that ensured his small-scale engravings and designs were given some of the characteristics of monumental art works.

Raine is particularly good on the crisp patterning evident in Blake's designs and paintings. Many distinguished scholars and connoisseurs from an earlier generation, such as C. H. Collins Baker, Laurence Binyon, Roger Fry, J. B. Manson and Basil de Sélincourt, dismissed Blake's restless contours as evidence of artistic vulgarity. Raine, by contrast, detects in Blake's process of composing through interlocking rhythms and lines evidence of a desire to assimilate Greek and Gothic influences into a single pictorial language. At the core of Blake's art, then, she discovers energetic activity: a world of sinewy and vigorous figures; forms that signify elastic power, as well as mental extension. Hence, 'line was, for Blake, above all an expression of energy. Every solid form can be seen as the imprint and product of a flow of energy, and it is certain that Blake saw line as energy, as the signature of life.' Time and again, she slashes through the dense undergrowth of Blake scholarship to offer sharp and powerful accounts of Blake's frenetic, kinetic style:

There is in Blake's minutest designs the sense that he is showing us... a world of the unhindered energy of spiritual life.... [He loved]

2 *Songs of Innocence*, c. 1825. Title-page.

the vital linear character of Gothic art.... The interlacing linear forms which adorn the pages of Songs of Innocence *are obviously influenced by medieval illuminated books; the character is the line, whose controlled freedom accompanies and surrounds the script in so harmonious a way. Even in the closely written pages of* Jerusalem, *tendrils creep into whatever space they can find, and insects, birds, fishes and serpents occupy those visual vacuums which Blake, like nature, abhors.*

These are virtuoso snapshots of two of Blake's most incandescent productions: *Songs of Innocence*, written, designed and executed in a moment of youthful ebullience in 1789; and *Jerusalem*, a cosmological argument in verse and design generated in the long period between 1804 and 1820. Both works, as noted by Raine, are prolific with life forms: they are portals into a rapturous world where everything is connected, a world where the artist-poet wants to become one with the multiple forms of life he captures. Blake's genius, Raine implies, is to create a new whole from the competing forces and experiences of human life.

Raine produces numerous tour de force readings of the forcefulness of imagery at once pantheistic, existential and ecstatic:

All Blake's most characteristic and beautiful images are of the minute: the wild thyme and meadowsweet... the worm, the ant, the grasshopper and spider; the little bird – lark or nightingale or robin red breast.... Life is neither great nor small.... Already in Songs of Innocence *Blake's figures have attained freedom from the gravitational forces which constrain material objects... a quality essentially Blakean, and shared by none of his contemporaries.*

This is a sparklingly intelligent explanation of an art that replaces physical space with mental space, a generous art of sensory enchantment that has life running through it.

Synthesis is another important aspect of Raine's critical model. Blake's works, she argues, belong on the same critical spectrum: free-standing designs relate to poetry, mythology and religion because Blake's imagination was fuelled by the idea of continuous vision, the conception of art as unified whole. She notes how *The Gates of Paradise* (1793), Blake's small book of emblems, relates to the Book of Job in the Old Testament, which deals with the mystery of human experience, and *The Four Zoas* (1797–1807), his own attempt to create a universal religion where dynamic particles are pushed into larger forms. The theme of *The Gates of Paradise*

4

3 *Jerusalem*, 1804–20. Title-page. The soul's metamorphosis is here completed in the beautiful winged figure of Jerusalem.

is Job's question: 'what is man?' Blake's answer, she suggests, is 'indicated by the symbol of metamorphosis. A caterpillar, symbol of "natural man", consumes the leaf of our native Druid tree, the oak; and on the other leaf, an infant sleeping in a chrysalis signifies the "second birth" of the "spiritual body" of humanity.' Then she turns her attention to the core images in *The Gates of Paradise*: 'The four Michelangelesque figures of Earth, Air, Fire and Water anticipate those Four Zoas whose mythological adventures form the substance of the Prophetic Books which were to follow. The number four... is by no means arbitrary, but corresponds to the four functions, or energies of the psyche: the "four living creatures" of the Book of Ezekiel and the Apocalypse of St John. To these Biblical... forms Blake was to give human attributes and features that are unforgettable.' These comments allow the reader to appreciate that Blake defined painting, printmaking and poetry as manifestations of interior cosmos, not as surrogates of external nature.

Blake's most powerful Prophetic Books – *The First Book of Urizen* (1794), *Milton* (1804–10) and *Jerusalem* (1804–20) – fascinate Raine. These 'cosmological picture books' are presented as visionary psychodramas, the disruption of temporal, pictorial and spatial conventions by expressions of 'the irresistible energy of life'. In *The First Book of Urizen* '[t]here are terrible and powerful depictions of constricted and distorted forms of life, suffering under the tyranny of Urizen's "laws of nature" and a morality based upon natural, not spiritual law. Spirits of life are drawn down from the region of consciousness which is, for every soul, its own place, into the dizzying abyss of time and space, Newton's "soul-shuddering vacuum" – in terms of life, "outside existence."' Here, in these grand, fiery productions, she discovers one of the sources of Blake's anti-materialist thinking:

For Blake, volume and weight belonged to the mechanistic concept of a natural world subject to the quantitative "laws of nature" as these operate in time and space.... Against the mechanistic view of nature, product of the natural mind of Urizen, Blake proclaimed life. Life is non-spatial and non-temporal; gravity does not weigh it down, nor bulk contain it. There are, for Blake's human figures, essentially two conditions – the unconfined freedom of unimpeded energy; and the constricted, fettered, weighted and cramped state of the prisoners of Urizen's universe of mechanized nature.

4 *The First Book of Urizen*, 1794. Title-page: Urizen with tables and book of law beneath the enrooted tree of nature.

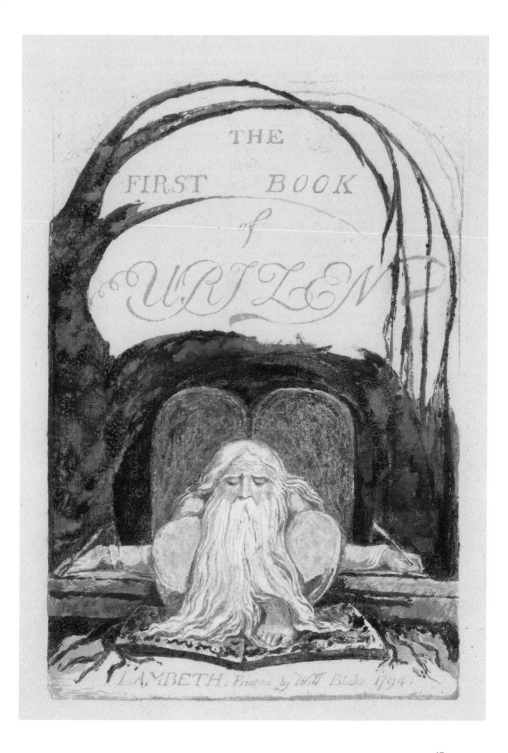

Urizen, Blake's personification of abstract reason and social regularity, broods on the abyss of History. A self-torturing and self-enclosing demiurge, this misanthropic sub-god is unable to understand the nature of human activity and is contrasted to the world of sensory perceptions, as exemplified by Los and Orc, Blake's main protagonists. The power governing Los and Orc is the imagination, which explains why they are represented as vital, elastic and undulating forms. Raine is especially good on the recursive nature of the imagery of Orc and Los: the way in which they represent the repeated application of energy to the problem of turning a world of parts into a universe of unified forms. As seen by her, Los and Orc are dynamic and fluid; Urizen is tense and marmoreal. In other words, different mentalities are given different bodily characteristics. Two versions of life are provided with their own distinct pictorial forms. For Los and Orc, life is expressive motion; for Urizen, life is measurement and stasis. Los and Orc embody uncurbed energy, a Dionysian immersion in the flux and efflux of the universe, a condition of eternal closeness to human experience; Urizen is imprisoned by the iron-cage logic of self-creation.

Raine, attentive to the expressiveness of the designs in *Jerusalem*, presents them as part of the actual living experience of the artist: 'The pages of *Jerusalem* are Blake at his most Blakean. The figures are executed in his fully evolved and simplified linear style... which is perfectly adapted to the novel technique Blake had invented. The linear decoration is itself calligraphic, merging harmoniously with the script. Grand, grotesque or lovely forms depict, as in some visual Divine Comedy, inner states of the soul.' Even at its most obscure, she hints, Blake's work feels human and alive, less the product of theory and system than of the mind and body.

In all these and similar cases, Raine reveals an ability to relate Blake's images to the governing themes of his worldview. Nor should we forget how uncommon it was at this time to discuss Blake, as Raine does, as a 'global' artist, someone who engaged with other cultures and their cultural forms. She notes how he incorporated Indian and Persian sources into his vision of a single, universal aesthetic. In the final decades of his life, she claims, Blake had 'reached the profounder perspectives of the Indian philosophies, of the Buddhist "wheel", on which all states are illusory, good and evil alike.' Blake's distinctiveness, as outlined in the following passage, is a way of addressing issues about vision, creativity and the interdependence of cultural worldviews:

The Last Judgment – *on the last of several versions of which Blake continued to work until the time of his death – has a character altogether unprecedented. Both this work and the closely related* Meditation among the Tombs *have a diagrammatic structure more common in Tibetan Buddhist art than in Christian iconography. The flowing figures, ascending to the radiant Christ Enthroned, or falling headlong into Hell as in Michelangelo's* Last Judgment, *seem less like individuals than cells circulating in the life-stream of cosmic life. While for single figures or groups of figures we can find parallels in works by Michelangelo, for the composition as a whole I know none later than the Gothic Middle Ages.*

In the liquid flow of the Blakean body Raine discovers a system of critical and pictorial fermentation of every element in the whole composition.

In sum, Raine's *William Blake* celebrates the creativity of a remarkable, and remarkably mercurial, genius. The underlying image of Raine's wonderful book is that Blake believed in the power of the imagination as a vector of human value. It is difficult to imagine a stronger reading of human personality and potential; it is impossible to ignore the timeliness of this generous vision to an age obsessed by the conviction that human values are best expressed in commercial interactions.

Colin Trodd

Introduction

Prophet, poet, painter, engraver – and according to tradition
a composer of melodies as well – Blake's unique greatness lies
in no single achievement, but in the whole of what he was, which
is more than the sum of all that he did. It belongs to a few great
imaginative minds that they can create a world which seems
to possess a reality, a coherence, a climate and atmosphere
of its own. Shakespeare, Dante, Dürer, Blake's own favourite
painters Fra Angelico, Claude and Michelangelo, seem to offer
us fragments of worlds whose bounds extend beyond any
of those portions their work has embodied; and that is one
of the delights of the kind of art I have in mind. Blake was such
an artist; and his work, as he believed, represents 'portions
of eternity' seen in imaginative vision. Blake himself writes of
'ever Existent Images' which may be seen 'by the Imaginative
Eye of Every one according to the situation he holds' –
a collective archetypal world whose reality is more credible
in our century than it was in his own. 'To different People it
appears differently, as everything else does.' Such art comes
from a source deeper than the individual experience of poet or
painter, and has a power of communication to that same level
in the spectator. To our superficial selves this is a source of the
'obscurity' of visionary art; to our deepest selves, of its lucidity.

Blake's work is on a small scale. His engravings and
illuminated pages are measurable in inches; his paintings, too,
tend to be small. But though he executed nothing monumental,
his imaginings were on the grandest scale. 'The Artist having
been taken in vision into the ancient republics, monarchies and
patriarchates of Asia, has seen those wonderful originals called
in the Sacred Scriptures the Cherubim, which were sculptured
and painted on the walls of Temples, Towers, Cities, Palaces and
erected in the highly cultivated states of Egypt, Moab, Edom,

Aram, among the Rivers of Paradise....' There is in Blake's minutest designs the sense that he is showing us a portion of those 'stupendous originals' of his vision, fragments of some unfallen world 'among the Rivers of Paradise' – a world of the unhindered energy of spiritual life. It is his gift of communicating his vision, rather than his technical accomplishment as a painter or engraver, that entitles Blake to so high a place.

'The Nature of Visionary Fancy, or Imagination, is very little Known....' Very little known because consciously possessed by few in our materialist civilization. Yet, with the aid of those who possess a faculty latent in all, we can participate through art in the enjoyment of an interior universe whose exploration is the theme of the religious and mythological art of all ages. For those to whom the outer world of the senses alone seems real, Blake, in common with all symbolic art, offers little; for others 'the end of a golden string' to thread the labyrinth of the psyche. Nor is this world cloudy or vague. 'A Spirit and a Vision are not, as the modern philosophy supposes, a cloudy vapour, or a nothing: they are organized and minutely articulated beyond all that the mortal and perishing nature can produce. He who does not imagine in stronger and better lineaments, and in stronger and better light than his perishing mortal eye can see, does not imagine at all. The painter of this work [his title-page for the poet Thomas Gray's *The Bard*] asserts that all his imaginations appear to him infinitely more perfect and more minutely organized than anything seen by his mortal eye. Spirits are organized men.'

Not content with defending the 'minute particulars' of vision, Blake pointed out that the copying of nature must lead in the end to loss of form: 'Men think they can Copy Nature as Correctly as I copy Imagination. This they will find Impossible, & all the Copiers or Pretended Copiers of Nature, from Rembrandt to Reynolds, Prove that Nature becomes to its Victim nothing but Blots & Blurs. Why are Copiers of Nature Incorrect, while Copiers of Imagination are Correct?'

Blake calls to witness the greatest art of the world, which depicts not what is seen by the 'mortal eye', but an imagined perfection: 'The connoisseurs and artists who have made objections to Mr B's mode of representing spirits with real bodies, would do well to consider that the Venus, the Minerva, the Jupiter, the Apollo, which they admire in Greek statues are all of them representatives of spiritual existences, of Gods immortal, to the mortal perishing organ of sight; and yet they are embodied and organized in solid marble.'

This is the Platonic view of art; and indeed Plotinus' *On the Beautiful* (in Thomas Taylor's translation) was early known to Blake. Essentially this is an aesthetics which sees

5 Illustration for Thornton's *Pastorals of Virgil*, 1821. 'Thenot Remonstrates with Collinet'.

wholes as determining parts, and ideas (which are wholes) as the organizing principles of the medium in which they are executed. Plotinus asks: 'What is the similitude between the beauties of sense, and that beauty which is divine?' And he answers that form gives unity to matter. 'Hence beauty is established in multitude, when the many is reduced to the one; and in this case it communicates itself both to the parts, and to the whole.... Thus at one and the same time it communicates itself to the whole building, and its several parts.... And hence body becomes beautiful, through the communion supernally proceeding from divinity.'

Blake's aesthetics belong to a greater extent than has generally been realized to the Greek revival; to which we shall presently return. But his earliest formation must first be considered.

Joseph of Arimathea
among The Rocks of Albion

Engraved by W Blake 1773 from an old Italian Drawing
This is One of the Gothic Artists who built the Cathedeals in what we call the Dark Ages
Wandering about in sheep skins & goat skins of whom the World was not worthy
such were the Christians
in all Ages
Michael Angelo Pinxit

6 *Joseph of Arimathea
among the Rocks of
Albion*, 1773. Engraved by
Blake after Michelangelo.

Chapter 1
Apprentice to Antiquity

Blake was first and last a Londoner. He was born on 28
November 1757, at 28 Broad (now Broadwick) Street, Golden
Square, the second child of 'a moderately prosperous hosier
of some twenty years' standing,' according to his Victorian
biographer, Alexander Gilchrist (1828–61). The poverty of
Blake's background and the meanness of his education have
been exaggerated. The Blake family occupied a spacious old
London house in a district half private houses, half respectable
shops, which was (Gilchrist again) in an 'ex-fashionable highly
respectable condition'. Blake was not 'a man of the people',
though his political views were radical, and in his youth
revolutionary. He belonged to the lower section of that stable
middle class which in fact produced most of the talent and
genius of the era. From the point of view of his family Blake was
a failure; his brother James, who inherited the family business,
stopped seeing William altogether in their later years.

It is true that Blake never went to school; but this probably
indicates, beside his own strong objection to being sent to
school, his father's enlightened tolerance of his son's artistic
bent. 'The Schoolboy' of *Songs of Innocence* is represented as a
victim of parental tyranny, not as for Gray, 'redolent of joy and
youth'. 'There is no use in education,' he said as an old man to
the diarist Henry Crabb Robinson (1775–1867); 'I hold it wrong –
34, 35   it is the great Sin.' An aphorism in *The Marriage of Heaven and
Hell* reflects Blake's thankfulness to have escaped the instruction
of the schoolmaster: 'Improvement makes strait roads; but the
crooked roads without Improvement are roads of Genius.'

'As soon as the child's hand could hold a pencil it began to
scrawl rough likenesses of man or beast, and make timid copies
of all the prints he came near', said Gilchrist. In those days
there was education or its want; there was no bad education,

no trash. The prints Blake saw as a child were of authentic works of art. At the age of ten, he was sent to the best and most fashionable preparatory school for young artists: Henry Pars' drawing-school in the Strand. Pars' younger brother, William, accompanied the architect Nicholas Revett (1721–1804) to Athens and Ionia, to study and draw 'ruined temple and mutilated statue, and to return with portfolios, a mine of wealth to cribbing "classic" architects – contemporary Chambers and future Soane.' Blake was later to make engravings of several of William Pars' plates for the famous Stuart and Revett portfolios of *The Antiquities of Athens and Ionia*. Blake's spirited Lapiths and Centaurs from the Parthenon frieze belong to that mythological world which was his native element.

Gilchrist reflects the current fashion of his own time in his evident regret that 'At Pars' school as much drawing was taught as is to be learned by copying plaster-casts of the Antique, but no drawing from the living figure.' But this suited Blake's natural preference for ideal form. Blake's father bought him a few casts: the Gladiator, the Hercules Farnese, the Venus de Medici, and wooden models of heads, hand and arm. He also gave him pocket money with which the boy, a haunter of print-dealers' shops and auction rooms, laid the foundation of a modest collection. A collector Blake remained throughout his life, though at a time of pressing poverty he sold his fine collection of prints. The landscape painter and printmaker Samuel Palmer (1805–81) recalled being taken to visit Blake, then an old man: 'I can never forget the evening when Mr Linnell took me to Blake's house, nor how the quiet hours passed with him in the examination of antique gems, choice pictures, and Italian prints of the sixteenth century.'

Blake was, in fact, from his boyhood to the end of his life, as highly cultured, not to say learned, in the visual arts as it is possible for any artist to be who was never able to visit Europe.

Pars' school had been founded by William Shipley (1715–1803), whose ideas also led to the founding of the Society of Arts; the Society's exhibition rooms, before its removal to the Adelphi over the way, were in the same building as the school. Blake must have seen there exhibitions of the most famous painters of the day. George Stubbs (1724–1806) exhibited there, and it is pleasing to imagine Blake as a boy enthralled by Stubbs' *Tiger*, conceived so much more in the spirit of Blake's famous poem than the toy-like creature of his own design.

43

At the age of fourteen Blake was apprenticed to James Basire (1730–1802), engraver to the Society of Antiquaries. In this, the middle-class caution of Blake's father the hosier is evident. The career of a painter was altogether too vague to appeal

to his practical sense; let his son at least be assured of a living
by his skill in a craft, and become a painter if he could. Perhaps
this decision was a mistaken one; it may be that Blake's great
imaginings were cramped somewhat by the limitations of
the engraver's art, which inevitably influenced his style as a
painter. But any loss to painting was to be compensated for by
the enrichment of the art of engraving by Blake's unsurpassed
161-8 *Illustrations of the Book of Job.* His craftsman's training was also,
almost accidentally, to put into his hands the technique which
enabled him to create his unique illuminated books. But the
strong and lasting influence of Basire's flat, old-fashioned and
formal style of engraving with the 'dot and lozenge' technique
he had inherited from George Vertue (1684–1756), engraver to the
Society of Antiquaries before him, may have had much to do
with Blake's later want of success in finding employment as an
engraver. The 'smooth' technique of William Woollett (1735–85),
Robert Strange (1721–92), Francesco Bartolozzi (1727–1815) and
his pupil Luigi Schiavonetti (1765–1810), so scorned by Blake,
was more agreeable to the new taste.

As Basire's apprentice Blake found himself in an
environment of Antiquity. The 'ancient republics, monarchies
and patriarchates of Asia' of his visions owed much to his
work for Basire on such books as Jacob Bryant's *New System of*
9 *Mythology* (1774–6), as famous a work in its day as James Frazer's
Golden Bough (1890). The artist, poet and editor Ruthven Todd
(1914–78) first discerned Blake's hand in several of the plates,
some of which contain details later discoverable in Blake's own
designs. In Plate 16 of his *Job* series, *When the Morning Stars*
1 *Sang Together*, the raised and crossed arms and parted feet are
a reflection of the frieze-figures of a Persian Temple of Mithras
illustrated in one of the Basire plates – possibly one Blake
himself worked on. The archaeological premises of Bryant's
monumental work were probably no more absurd than many
since: that all the pantheons of Antiquity must be related to
the eight human beings who survived the Deluge in Noah's
7, 8 Ark. Ruthven Todd first put side by side the moon-ark of the
tail-piece of volume three of Bryant's *Mythology* and the several
moon-arks of Blake's mythological works. It was to Bryant that
Blake owed his revelation – a bold one at that time – that 'the
antiquities of every Nation under Heaven, is no less sacred than
that of the Jews. They are the same thing, as Jacob Bryant and
all antiquaries have proved.... All had originally one language,
and one religion: this was the religion of Jesus, the everlasting
Gospel. Antiquity preaches the Gospel of Jesus.' The *Mythology*
was a gold-mine, upon which Blake drew in the composition
of his own pantheon of mythological lore; a universal language

(as Bryant himself had understood) of the human imagination, with dialectical variations according to time, place, and local tradition.

Blake's dreams of the colossal were perhaps in part a reflection of a moment at which there was talk of a colossal statue by the sculptor John Flaxman (1755–1826) at Greenwich (never carried out); but they must also have reflected those Persian temples and sculptures of Greece and Egypt which had impressed his imagination during his seven years in Basire's workshop. 'Those wonderful originals seen in my visions, were some of them one hundred feet in height; some were painted as pictures, and some carved as basso relievos, and some as groupes of statues, all containing mythological and recondited meaning, where more is meant than meets the eye. The Artist wishes it was now the fashion to make such monuments, and then he should not doubt of having a national commission to execute these two Pictures [the Spiritual Forms of Lord Nelson and William Pitt, 1805–9] on a scale that is suitable to the grandeur of the nation.'

Two years after Blake's apprenticeship, kindly Basire, to get him out of the way of two troublesome new apprentices, sent

7 LEFT Moon-ark. *Jerusalem*, 1804–20.
8 OPPOSITE ABOVE Moon-ark and dove of peace from Jacob Bryant's *New System of Mythology*, 1774–6, probably by Blake.
9 OPPOSITE BELOW Temple of Mithras from Jacob Bryant's *New System of Mythology*, 1774–6.

And these may be observed in the names of Deities, terms of
worship, and titles of honour, which prevail among nations
widely separated : who for ages have had no connexion. The
like may be found in the names of pagodas and temples ;
and of sundry other objects, which will present themselves to
the traveller. Even America would contribute to this purpose.
The more rude the monuments, the more ancient they may
possibly prove ; and afford a greater light upon inquiry.

Thus far I have proceeded in the explanation and proof of
the system, in which I first engaged. Should any thing still
remain, which can afford a further illustration, it must be
deferred for a season.

F   I   N   I   S.

Plate V.

Temple of Mithras Petræus in the Mountains of Persia. From Le Brun.

him to make drawings of monuments and buildings in the various old churches of London, and especially at Westminster Abbey. Blake was always grateful to Basire for this opportunity to study Gothic architecture and sculpture. Basire was at that time working on the plates of the *Archaeologia* and the *Vetusta Monumenta* journals of the Society of Antiquaries. According to Gilchrist, Blake engraved some of the plates which bear the name of Basire, among them those of Edward III, Queen Philippa, and Aveline of Lancaster. The art historian Anthony Blunt (1907–83) also attributed to Blake the watercolour copies of the murals of two English kings in Westminster Abbey, known as Henry III and King Sebert, which were engraved in the second volume of *Vetusta Monumenta.* Blake's work may also be traced in the *Memoir* of Thomas Hollis (1780); and in Richard Gough's two-volume *Sepulchral Monuments*, not published until 1786 and 1796. Gilchrist records that Blake discovered for himself, then or later, the important part colour once played in Gothic churches; in his imagination the Abbey once more became 'a radiant Temple of God' which was 'now a bleached dishonoured skeleton'.

Blake's lifelong love of Gothic art dates from this time; almost by chance he was able to study a style which was already becoming fashionable, notably through Horace Walpole (1717–97) and his friend the poet Thomas Gray (1716–71). For Blake it was spiritual affinity rather than fashion which drew him to the aristocratic linear style of Late Gothic sculpture. He discovered in this noble art the central tradition of Catholic Christian art as it flourished in England at a time when the English style was a living branch of the great European tradition.

For Blake, the Gothic style was the Christian style *par excellence*; a view John Ruskin (1819–1900) was later to share, but not one current in the eighteenth century. Commenting on Virgil in 1820 Blake wrote: 'Grecian is Mathematical Form: Gothic is living form, Mathematic Form is eternal in the Reasoning Memory: Living Form is Eternal Existence.' In Christopher Wren's St Paul's Cathedral he saw a monument of Deism, the 'natural religion' of the Enlightenment, of 'Newton's Pantocrator', demiurge of the mechanistic universe of science. Plate 32 of Blake's *Jerusalem* shows beside Vala 'the Goddess Nature' the dome of St Paul's, while the soul-figure, Jerusalem, and her children keep guard over his beloved Westminster Abbey. In 1773, when Blake was not yet sixteen, he made

10 *King Sebert*, 1778. Blake's copy of a mural in Westminster Abbey, later engraved in *Vetusta Monumenta*.

a drawing after Michelangelo (which he later engraved) entitled *Joseph of Arimathea among the Rocks of Albion*; below, he wrote: 'This is One of the Gothic Artists who Built the Cathedrals in what we call the Dark Ages, Wandering about in sheep skins & goat skins, of whom the World was not worthy; such were the Christians in all Ages.' Only Blake could have seen a Gothic hero in Michelangelo's soldier.

'Let them look at Gothic Figures & Gothic Buildings & not talk of Dark Ages or of any Age. Ages are all Equal. But Genius is Always Above the Age,' he wrote in the margins of Joshua Reynolds' *Discourses on Painting*. In his poem 'I saw a monk of Charlemaine', included in the preface to *Jerusalem*, Chapter 3, Blake challenged the current fashion of the Enlightenment which held medieval Christendom in contempt. Voltaire, Rousseau and Gibbon, he says, 'charge the poor Monks & Religious with being the causes of War, while you aquit & flatter the Alexanders & Caesars, the Lewis's & Fredericks who alone are its causes & its actors.' 'The Classics! it is the Classics & not Goths nor Monks, that Desolate Europe with Wars.'

The intention of Gothic portrait-sculpture was not naturalistic, nor the reproduction of every detail and blemish of the physical form, but rather the expression of the essence of the spiritual tenant of the earthly body, and, in addition, of kingship, sanctity, military courage or feminine grace, as such. So Blake, too, was to conceive portraiture. His many Bible illustrations represent the lineaments of some spiritual state, whether good or evil, and as such invite comparison with the sculptures of Chartres, and Gothic depictions of the lineaments of human feeling. Esteemed historian of art and architecture Nikolaus Pevsner (1902–83) spoke of Blake's 'flaming line' as distinctively English. The sinuous flowing lines of his drapery, the elongation of his figures, derive from the Decorated or Flamboyant Gothic architecture and sculpture which he knew in Westminster Abbey. The static and monumental was not natural to Blake; yet when he depicts death it is in terms of the calm recumbence of the figures on the royal tombs.

More congenial to his natural bent was the vital linear character of Gothic art, whether in the human form, the foliate decoration of stone, or the pages of illuminated books. For Blake, the essence of art was the line: 'firm and determinate lineaments unbroken by shadows'. 'The Beauty proper for sublime art is lineaments, or forms and features that are capable of being receptacles of intellect.' This description fits no style so well as the Gothic; it was Blake's implicit standard of comparison with that 'Chiaro Oscuro' which he hated: 'Such art of losing the outlines is the art of Venice and Flanders; it loses

11 *The Death of Saint Joseph*, 1803.

all character, and leaves what some people call expression; but this is a false notion of expression; expression cannot exist without character as its stamina; and neither character nor expression can exist without firm and determinate outline.' Of colouring, he wrote that this 'does not depend on where the colours are put, but where the lights and darks are put, and all depends on Form or Outline, on where that is put; where that is wrong, the colouring never can be right; and it is always wrong in Titian and Correggio, Rubens and Rembrandt.' A summary dismissal, by any standard.

The linear style is, in fact, characteristic of religious art; and always Blake insists that the 'spirits', whether of men or gods, should be 'organized', within a 'determinate and bounding form'.

The 'tendrils of the wandering vine', the interlacing linear forms which adorn the pages of *Songs of Innocence* (1789), are obviously influenced by medieval illuminated books; here again, the character is the line, whose controlled freedom accompanies and surrounds the script in so harmonious a way. Even in the closely written pages of *Jerusalem* (1804–20), tendrils creep into whatever space they can find, and insects, birds, fishes and serpents occupy those visual vacuums which Blake, like nature, abhors. The formalized vine leaves have the look of Gothic foliage. On many plates the human figures, too, are

13

formalized into decoration in a way reminiscent of the fantasies of Gothic stonemasons. In Blake's Notebook (and sometimes later elaborated in his designs), we find letters and formalized designs obviously derived from Gothic lettering, or from corbels and capitals of Gothic sculpture.

Blake's admiration for Gray, for Thomas Chatterton (1752–70), for Thomas Percy's *Reliques of Ancient English Poetry* (1765) and for early British history was consistent with his Gothic enthusiasm. His first-hand, exact knowledge of Gothic sculpture and painting was incomparably greater than that of Horace Walpole or William Beckford (1760–1844), whose 'follies' in the Gothic style were mere fantasies. Blake often expressed himself wildly on subjects he knew exactly, in contrast with those measured Augustan sentences, adopted by other writers of his time, which lend weight to often superficial knowledge.

One might guess that Blake's early passion for Shakespeare was a consequence of his acquaintance with sculptured lineaments of the kings and queens of the historical plays. *Poetical Sketches*, his earliest work, written between 1769 and 1777, contains fragments of historical drama in rough-hewn Shakespearian blank verse. Still more fruitful was the influence of Shakespeare's lyrics, already evident in these early poems, and soon to flower in *Songs of Innocence and of Experience* – the most vitally 'linear' lyric poetry since Shakespeare himself. So it is with the 'crooked roads of Genius' – one vital interest leads to another: the royal tombs to Shakespeare, and both (ultimately)

12 'Gothic' designs from Blake's Notebook, c. 1793.

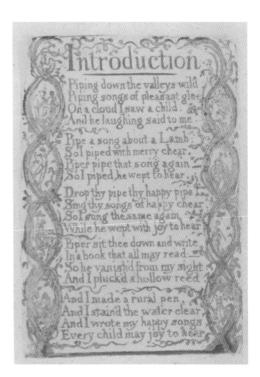

13 *Songs of Innocence*, 1789. Introduction.

to Blake's own national myth of 'the Giant Albion', the collective Being of the English nation. Blake's historical sense was derived less from history books (though he read Froissart, Geoffrey of Monmouth and other such medieval writers) than immediately from the great works of earlier ages. His learning was none the less exact and extensive for being that of a draughtsman rather than a man of books.

It was no doubt under the inspiration of English history, whose atmosphere he had absorbed during his long hours in the company of England's dead kings and queens, that Blake, as Basire's apprentice and immediately afterwards, worked on elaborate historical compositions somewhat in the style of Angelica Kauffmann (1741–1807) and John Hamilton Mortimer (1740–79): *The Penance of Jane Shore, Edward and Eleanor, The Ordeal of Queen Emma, The Death of Earl Godwin.* Later, art historian Anthony Blunt (1907–83) had no high opinion of these productions: 'As a painter, if he had died at the age of thirty [Blake] would be thought of as a minor and rather incompetent member of a group of artists in revolt against Sir Joshua Reynolds and the official doctrine of the Royal Academy.' He describes this current manner as 'on the border-line between Late Rococo

14

14 *The Penance of Jane Shore in St Paul's Church*, c. 1793. As the mistress of Edward IV Jane Shore was forced to walk in penance in St Paul's Church. Blake's sympathy is apparent in this drawing. He himself thought well of this work, and included it in his exhibition of 1809.

and Neoclassicism'; and points out that in costume, Blake, like the painters whom he imitated, 'followed contemporary stage productions of Shakespeare's plays dealing with medieval themes, which consisted of a mixture of Elizabethan and eighteenth-century elements with the occasional addition of a medieval suit of armour rendered with considerable freedom'.

Blake left Basire's studios at the end of his seven years' apprenticeship at the age of twenty-one, and set to work to earn his living as an engraver. The descent into the world of commercial art must have come as a rude awakening for the young man who had dreamed away seven industrious years among the royal tombs and still more ancient monuments of Antiquity. He continued to live in his father's house, but was now engaged on plates for the *Novelist's Magazine,* the *Ladies' Magazine* and the like. For a time he enrolled himself as a student at the newly founded Royal Academy, which was then (in Gilchrist's words) 'in an uncomfortable chrysalis condition, having had to quit its cramped lodgings in Somerset House (pulled down in 1775); and awaiting the completion of the new building in which more elbow room was to be provided.' But it was not the cramped physical conditions which irked Blake so much as the cramped imaginative environment. Besides drawing from the Antique, life drawing was the order of the day, and this, to Blake, was anathema: 'Natural Objects always did & now do weaken, deaden & obliterate Imagination in Me.' So he wrote many years later in his manuscript notes on Wordsworth. Gothic stylization had formed his taste to another conception of art, and in the Academy drawing school he was out of his element. No doubt his antipathy to Joshua Reynolds (1723–92), first president of the Royal Academy, dates from those uneasy months. As a man of fifty, he wrote scathing annotations in his copy of Reynolds' *Discourses on Painting.* With the illusory triumph of a *pensée d'escalier,* he describes a clash with George Michael Moser (1706–83), the first Keeper of the Academy, who naturally assumed that his words would be gospel to such obscure young men as William Blake: 'I was once looking over the Prints from Raffael & Michael Angelo in the Library of the Royal Academy. Moser came to me & said: "You should not Study these old Hard, Stiff & Dry, Unfinish'd Works of Art – Stay a little & I will shew you what you should Study." He then went & took down Le Brun's and Rubens' *Galleries.* How I did secretly Rage! I also spoke my Mind... I said to Moser, "These things that you call Finish'd are not Even Begun: how then can they be Finish'd? The Man who does not know The Beginning never can know the End of Art."'

In particular Blake hated 'that infernal machine called Chiaro Oscuro, in the hands of Flemish and Venetian Demons'. Against 'blotting and blurring demons' Blake waged a lifelong war, though he was forced, on his own admission, to give ground a little by 'the spirit of Titian': 'The spirit of Titian was particularly active in raising doubts concerning the possibility of executing without a model, and when once he had raised the doubt, it became easy for him to snatch away the vision time after time, for, when the Artist took his pencil to execute his ideas, his power of imagination weakened so much and darkened, that memory of nature, and of Pictures of the various schools possessed his mind... like walking in another man's style, or speaking, or looking in another man's style and manner, unappropriate and repugnant to your own individual character....'

Rubens, too, forced Blake's reluctant admiration: 'Rubens is a most outrageous demon, and by infusing the remembrance of his Pictures and style of execution, hinders all power of individual thought: so that the man who is possessed by his demon loses all admiration for any other Artist but Rubens....'

Samuel Palmer rectifies our picture of Blake as a narrow fanatic, unwilling to enjoy art in styles other than those in which he himself found nourishment: 'Those who may have read some strange passages in his *Catalogue*, written in irritation, and probably in haste, will be surprised to hear, that in conversation he was anything but sectarian or exclusive, finding sources of delight throughout the whole range of art; while, as a critic, he was judicious and discriminating.'

Palmer is recalling Blake as an old man; perhaps his tastes had broadened with time. But the impression we gain is that it was not so much Rubens and Titian, as their academic admirers, who aroused Blake's prophetic rage.

Among Blake's early friends were the 'wild' Swiss painter Henry Fuseli (1741–1825), and James Barry (1741–1806), who executed the fine mural paintings in the Royal Society of Arts, and who shared Blake's passion for Michelangelo. Anthony Blunt pointed out several close parallels between Blake's early work and that of Barry, whose *King Lear*, and *Job*, in particular, seem to have fired his imagination. Barry was an Irishman, a Catholic, and a visionary, and their friendship may provide a clue to Blake's sympathy (minimized by Gilchrist, his biographer) with the 'Romish Church'. The anti-Catholic Gordon Riots of 1780 made a deep impression on Blake, who always championed the cause of the persecuted. Blake's revolutionary sympathies have been so often recorded

15 Illustration for Thornton's *Virgil*, 1821. 'Thenot under a Fruit Tree.'

(and exaggerated) that this less often noted sympathy seems worth mentioning here. Our greatest Christian artist never went to church, but 'ever professed his preference of the Church to any sort of sectarianism'. 'He used to ask how it was that we heard so much of priestcraft, and so little of soldier-craft and lawyercraft' – so Samuel Butler recollected. He had a 'preference for ecclesiastical governments', among which he explicitly admired the Papacy. The *Life* of the sixteenth-century Spanish mystic St Teresa was among his favourite books, and he admired the French Quietist Jeanne Guyon (1648–1717), and her admirer, the theologian François Fénelon (1651–1715).

Such views are not strange when we consider that Blake was saturated in the greatest art of the medieval Catholic tradition; the many examples of Tudor vulgarity which deface Westminster Abbey found no place in his admiration.

Chapter 2
'The Lost Art of the Greeks'

So strong was the influence upon Blake of the Gothic style that another, and apparently contrary influence, that of the Greek Revival, has tended to be overlooked. But, with that infallible gift of genius for being open to the significant – which is not necessarily to say, the fashionable – influences at any moment of time, Blake found himself at its centre. In about 1782 Thomas Stothard (1755–1834), an older fellow-engraver, introduced Blake to John Flaxman, then newly married and living at 27 Wardour Street, not far from Broad Street and Golden Square. Blake came for a time to share his friend's enthusiasm for Greek art. With the same whole-heartedness he showed in his love of the Gothic, we find Blake in 1799 writing to another Greek enthusiast and one of the founders of the National Gallery, George Cumberland of Bristol (1754–1848), that his 'Genius or Angel' was guiding his inspiration to the fulfilment of 'the purpose for which alone I live, which is... to renew the lost Art of the Greeks'. He was later to write very hard things about 'the Greek and Roman slaves of the sword', but his love for Greek art and Greek mythology remained. Blake and Flaxman shared a passion for the linear, the 'clear and determinate outline', though Flaxman drew chiefly on Greek models, Blake on the Gothic. Blake's lifelong love of 'the human form divine', the nude of art unblurred by the nudity of nature, is in part a reflection of his undiminished admiration of those Antique sculptures he had delighted to copy in his student days, and later discovered in the company of Flaxman.

Blake married in 1782. His wife, Catherine Boucher (1762–1831), was the illiterate daughter of a Battersea market-gardener. He married beneath him, and his father who had, after all, done everything in his power to encourage his gifted son, was displeased. William left his father's house under a cloud to set

16 Catherine Blake's drawing of
William at the age of twenty-eight.

up house with Catherine at 23 Green Street, Leicester Fields;
'in which Fields or Square, the junior branches of Royalty had
lately abode', besides 'the great Hogarth'.

Just as Blake's want of education has been exaggerated, so,
probably, has his happiness in his marriage. That Catherine
was to be no help to him socially probably did not trouble him.
But he had married her on the rebound from an unrequited
passion for a dark-eyed girl of whom we can surmise only (from
a song in *Poetical Sketches*) that she was his social superior:

I curse my stars in bitter grief and woe,
That made my love so high, and me so low.

After the death of his father in 1784, Blake moved back to Broad
Street, setting up at No. 27, next door to his old home (where his
brother James had now inherited the hosiery business). He took
a former fellow-apprentice, James Parker, as partner, and his
own talented younger brother, Robert, as a pupil and member
of his household. For two and a half happy, if financially
unsuccessful, years, this much-loved brother was an intellectual
companion; but Robert Blake died, at the age of twenty or a
little more: the greatest personal bereavement in Blake's life.

On the internal evidence of *Songs of Experience* and other poems unpublished, it seems Blake began to find his marriage irksome; no doubt Catherine bored him, and she was childless. There is mention of 'a handmaiden' whom Blake at one time wished to introduce into the household, a practice permitted (as Desirée Hirst described in her book on Blake, *Hidden Riches*, 1964) by the Swedenborgian Society, of which Blake and his wife were members. On the slender internal evidence of the poem 'Mary', and *Visions of the Daughters of Albion* (Blake's equivalent of Milton's tract on divorce), it is just possible that Blake was attracted to writer and campaigner for women's rights Mary Wollstonecraft (1759–97), whose views on free love he shared. To judge from the bitterness of some of the *Songs of Experience*, and, still more, from the evidence of the unpublished poem 'William Bond' (and also from the guarded Gilchrist), it seems that the trouble in Blake's marriage was serious. Whether because of Mary Wollstonecraft or some other woman, there was a time of sorrow for both William and Catherine:

'O William, if thou dost another Love
Dost another Love better than poor Mary,
Go & take that other to be thy Wife
And Mary Green shall her Servant be.'

The conclusion is a triumph of mutual generosity: William Bond is won by his wife's sublime gesture of renunciation, and in his turn renounces his intention of leaving her. The poem ends on a note never touched upon by any poet of merely romantic love:

Seek Love in the Pity of other's Woe,
In the gentle relief of another's care,
In the darkness of night & the winter's snow,
In the naked & outcast, Seek Love there!

In their later years Mr and Mrs Blake lived in a simple harmony which won the respect of those young painters for whom Blake was a master not only of painting, but of the good life.

It was during the early years of Blake's friendship with him that Flaxman persuaded Josiah Wedgwood (1730–95) to make his famous replicas of the Portland Vase, the first of his many replicas and imitations of Greco-Roman vases. In a letter dated 5 February 1784, Flaxman urged Wedgwood to come to London

17, 18 From Blair's *The Grave*, 1808. OPPOSITE *The Soul exploring the Recesses of the Grave;* OVERLEAF *Death's Door.*

The Soul exploring the recesses of the Grave.

London Published Mar 1st 1813, by R. H. Cromek, 64 Strand.

Death's Door

'Tis but a Night, a long and moonless Night,
We make the Grave our Bed, and then are gone!

London, Published March 1, 1813, by R. Ackermann, Strand.

to 'see Sir Wm. Hamilton's vase, it is the finest production of Art brought to England'. In 1790, after the vase had been purchased by the Duke of Portland in 1786, several replicas were made at the Wedgwood pottery and exhibited at the Wedgwood showrooms in Green Street. In 1791 Erasmus Darwin (grandfather of the naturalist and friend of the Wedgwoods) published in Part 1 of his *Botanic Garden* a long essay in which he argued, probably mistakenly, that the vase figures are emblems of the Eleusinian Mysteries. Blake made the fine set of engravings for Darwin's work, and must, therefore, have had either the original vase or one of the replicas in his workroom for some time. The theme of *The Soul exploring the Recesses of the Grave*, used by Blake in his illustrations to Robert Blair's poem *The Grave* (1743; Blake's illustrations published 1808) and in several later compositions, certainly owes something to the second compartment of the Portland Vase. In one of the illustrations to *The Grave*, the vigorous male figure above bears some resemblance to the youth entering the Kingdom of Hades through what is (according to Darwin's interpretation) 'the door of death'. And in the Frontispiece to *Jerusalem*, while

17, 18

19

20

19 The Portland Vase, second compartment, engraved by Blake for Darwin's *Botanic Garden*, 1791.

the door is Gothic (it suggests, indeed, one of those low doors into crypt or cloister that Blake knew well in Westminster Abbey), the figure's tentative advance still carries a suggestion of the youth on the Portland Vase. We can see it in the drawing of the left foot, and, perhaps (taken from another figure on the vase), the right foot cut off just above the ankle; and

20 *Jerusalem*, 1804–20. Frontispiece: Los exploring the Recesses of the Grave.

21 *Fertilization of Egypt*, after Henry Fuseli, from Erasmus Darwin's *Botanic Garden*, 1791.

(if we mentally remove the eighteenth-century hat) the eager profile of the face, half afraid, half exalted with wonder.

Also for Darwin's book, Blake engraved Fuseli's drawing of *Fertilization of Egypt*, into which he introduced a figure of his own invention: an aged figure with vast beard and outstretched arms who advances like a low cloud across the heavens. Anthony Blunt discovered the Roman relief of Jupiter Pluvius which was clearly Blake's inspiration, and the source of what was to be one of his favourite depictions of the aged figure of his own (often 'weeping') demiurge Urizen. Flaxman in one of his Dante illustrations derives from the same figure, or from Blake, or both.

In 1791 Blake made from drawings by William Pars a set of engravings from the Parthenon frieze for Stuart's and Revett's *Antiquities of Athens and Ionia*. In accepting the commission offered him by William Reveley, Blake wrote: 'he is glad to embrace the offer of engraving such beautiful things & will do what he can by the end of January.' Flaxman spent seven years in Italy between 1787 and 1794, returning with his famous series of drawings for Homer, Aeschylus and Dante. His plates for the *Odyssey*, said to have been lost on the voyage to England, were re-engraved by Blake.

Certain other visual themes are reminiscent of Greek
145   sculpture or reliefs. The veiled figure of Vala (*Jerusalem*,
Plate 32) recalls a convention of Greco-Roman iconography
in which the long veil is held loosely above the head. Blake's
friend George Cumberland published, in 1795, a series of
22   drawings illustrating the story of Cupid and Psyche; eight
of these Blake engraved, including one in which Psyche's
veil floats above her somewhat in the manner of the figure
of Vala (probably so named from her attribute, the Greek
peplos, or veil). The absurd butterfly wings of Cumberland's
23   Psyche can be recognized in the fairy-figure illustrating
Blake's own 'Infant Joy.' But on the title-page of *Jerusalem*,
the wings of the soul have become gorgeous with sun, moon
and stars. Caterpillar, chrysalis and butterfly is a Greek
24   symbolic theme to which Blake often returned. There are, in
Bryant's *Mythology*, emblems from antique gems, seals and
intaglios representing this widespread Hellenistic emblem
25   of the 'second birth' of the soul. The unforgettable first
emblem of *The Gates of Paradise*, depicting the caterpillar of
the 'natural man' and the dreaming infant soul in its chrysalis

22 *The Conjugal Union
of Cupid*, 'From an
Original Invention by
G. Cumberland Engd.
by W. Blake', 1794.

23 TOP LEFT *Songs of Innocence*, 1789. 'Infant Joy.'
24 TOP RIGHT Greco-Roman seals from Jacob Bryant's *New System of Mythology*,
1774–6, with typical emblems of metamorphosis.
25 ABOVE RIGHT 'What is Man!' Frontispiece to *The Gates of Paradise*, 1793. 'The Sun's
Light when he unfolds it/Depends on the Organ that beholds it.'

of metamorphosis, derives no doubt from these, or from some of those antique gems in Blake's own collection, mentioned by Samuel Palmer, besides literary sources.

Cumberland's *Thoughts on Outline*, published in 1796, exalts 'the inestimable value of chaste outline' characteristic of ancient art, a phrase suggestive of Blake's influence, or of a point of view current in their circle. Cumberland remained a friend to Blake to the end of his life.

Thomas Taylor the Platonist (1758–1835), known as 'the English Pagan', was a friend of George Cumberland's, and Blake must have known him too; Taylor is probably 'Sipsop the Pythagorean' of the satirical fragment *An Island in the Moon*. Cumberland was not the only probable link between Blake and Taylor: Taylor gave a series of lectures on Platonic philosophy 'before a distinguished audience' at Flaxman's house shortly before Flaxman's departure for Italy in 1787, and Blake most likely attended. Taylor's friend, William Meredith, has described Taylor giving Blake a lesson on the fifth proposition of Euclid: 'Taylor was going through the demonstration, but was interrupted by Blake, exclaiming "ah never mind that – what's the use of going to prove it. Why I see with my own eyes that it is so, & do not require any proof to make it clearer."' Blake's

mythological painting illustrating the Neoplatonist Porphyry's (*c.* 234–*c.* 305) *De Antro Nympharum* (Taylor's translation), made many years later, in 1821, gives the impression (as do the *Illustrations of the Book of Job* made about the same time) of a symbolic theme long considered – one, indeed, which runs through his own poetry and belongs to the very structure of his thought. The painting depicts Porphyry's myth of the 'descent' of souls into generation, and their 'return': the life-cycle as conceived by the Neoplatonic philosophers. The figure of Athene (who stands behind Odysseus) is veiled and draped in the Classical manner. The four horses which draw the goddess Leucothea (and still more, those drawing the sun god in his car) recall the Parthenon frieze, while the winged figures on the upper right of the picture, bearing urns on their heads, suggest, perhaps, the caryatids of the Acropolis. Blake was remembering themes current in his circle in the 1790s.

The strongest Greek influence on Blake was not visual but mythological. Since it often happened that he reclothed Greek themes in modern (or Gothic) dress, the extent to which he participated in the Greek Revival has not been generally recognized. The title-page of *Songs of Experience* (1794) shows the recumbent dead executed in the style of the royal tombs, but the underlying myth is the Platonic theme: that men 'die' into this world from a kingdom of immortal life, 'For who

26 *Tiriel: Har and Heva Bathing: Mnetha Looking*, 1785–9.
27 *Tiriel supporting the Dying Myratana and Cursing His Sons*, 1786–9. **49**

knows whether to live be not to die, and to die, to live?' Blake uses the same Gothic depiction, in the same Platonic sense, in his illustrations to Blair's *The Grave.*

'The Little Girl Lost' and 'The Little Girl Found' (first included in *Songs of Innocence* and later transferred to *Songs of Experience*) are a retelling of the most famous secret religious rites of ancient Greece, the Greater and Lesser Mysteries of Eleusis – the descent of the Kore into Hades, and the nine mystic nights of the Mother's search for her child. The poems are based upon Thomas Taylor's *Dissertation on the Eleusinian and Bacchic Mysteries* (1790), and also upon the figures of the Portland Vase and Erasmus Darwin's account of them. Many of Blake's themes, both mythological and philosophic, especially in his early Prophetic Books (the Lambeth Books), derive from Taylor's writings and translations.

26, 27 The dramatic poem *Tiriel*, written in about 1789, is a strange blend of Greek and alchemical themes with Rousseau's and Mary Wollstonecraft's new theories of education. The figure of Tiriel himself has many affinities with the Sophoclean Oedipus Coloneus; and Blake's (typically tenuous) plot suggests the conflict between aged Oedipus and the sons whom he cursed. Needless to say Blake's sympathies are entirely with the sons. The illustrations of *Tiriel* reflect Blake's Neoclassical interests: there are suggestions of Classical architecture in several plates, and the costumes – those of Hela and Tiriel in Plate VII for example – are more or less Greek in intention.

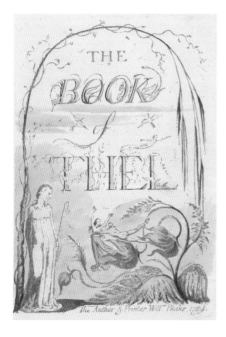

28 *The Book of Thel*, 1789. Title-page.

Chapter 3
A New Mode of Printing

Poetical Sketches, Blake's first collection of poems (including some written in his boyhood), was published in 1783 through the patronage of a Mrs Mathew, a clergyman's wife who had 'taken up' Flaxman, and, on Flaxman's introduction, for a time extended her patronage to Blake. Mrs Mathew and her husband paid half the cost of printing Blake's poems, Flaxman apparently paying the rest. Gilchrist records that Mrs Mathew used to read Homer to Flaxman; but when it became apparent that Blake came not to learn but to teach, his welcome in Mrs Mathew's circle of admirers became less warm. Blake did not suffer patrons gladly, and the comedy of Mrs Mathew was to be repeated fifteen years later (with Flaxman again the well-meaning intermediary) in the episode of his three years' employment by the poet and country squire William Hayley (1745–1820). Blake was never an easy man socially. 'A mental Prince', he was proud, argumentative, and violently opposed to current fashion, in his art and his philosophic and religious ideas alike. His only tenable role in his world was that of the venerated teacher he became, in his old age, to the group of young painters known as the 'Shoreham Ancients'.

Artists who work for quick success must rise on a tide of fashion, or possess social graces and tact, or private means. Blake, who was ready to speak his mind to Moser on the subject of 'Venetian and Flemish demons', was 'a priest and king in his own household', but no courtier. A radical in politics, Swedenborgian in religion, with no interest whatever in making money, Blake was clearly destined for worldly failure. He was a man of tireless industry; he carried out his commissions as an engraver laboriously and conscientiously. But his thoughts were elsewhere.

From whatever combination of causes and circumstances, it came about that he was without a publisher for his subsequent books of verse. True, *The French Revolution*, an unreadable verse narrative and commentary whose turgid style recalls Thomas Carlyle's later prose work of the same name, was actually set up in type by Blake's friend and employer Joseph Johnson (1738–1809), the radical bookseller; but it was then considered too dangerous to publish.

The political and moral subversiveness of his early works provides one possible explanation of how Blake came to be his own publisher; but were there deeper reasons? Did he wish to produce books of an entirely new kind? Books as beautiful as some medieval psalter, the words enhanced by decoration of design and colour? The bibliographer and scholar Geoffrey Keynes (1887–1982) pointed out that the germinal idea of such books was already in Blake's mind when in about 1784 he wrote his dramatic farce, *An Island in the Moon*. The first part is missing from the manuscript of a passage which begins abruptly:

"'... thus Illuminating the Manuscript."
"'Ay," said she, "that would be excellent."
"'Then," said he, "I would have all the writing Engraved instead of Printed, and at every other leaf a high-finish'd print – all in three Volumes folio – & sell them a hundred pounds apiece. They would print off two thousand."'

Far from being a child of necessity, the idea was to make a great deal of money.

Keynes thought that this idea may have been suggested to Blake by George Cumberland, who early in 1784 wrote to his brother Richard with 'the enclosed specimen of my new mode of Printing – it is the amusement of an evening and is capable of printing 2000 if I wanted them – you see here one page which is executed as easily as writing and the cost is trifling.' Cumberland's letter goes on to point out that you need print no more than are needed at one time, and that the copper plates can be used again – the only difficulty being that work of this kind can only be read with the aid of a looking-glass, as the letters are reversed. 'However we have a remedy for this defect also,' he adds. Can this 'we' conceivably have included Blake, or may Blake have been the real originator of the idea? Cumberland concludes: 'the expense of this page is 1/6 without reckoning time, wh. was never yet worth much to authors, and the Copper is worth 1/– again when cut up. In my next I will tell you more and make you also an engraver of this sort, till when keep it to yourself.'

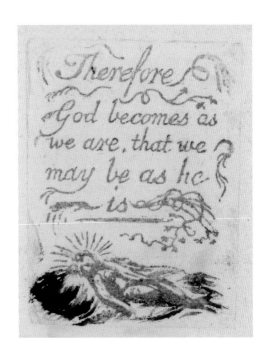

29 From *There is no Natural Religion*, c. 1788. Blake's first illuminated book.

Blake first used the method of 'illuminated printing' in about 1788. Three small tractates entitled *There is no Natural Religion* seem to have been his first experiments in this art. They are crudely executed in comparison with his later work, very small (copper was expensive), and simple in design. The title-page of *Songs of Innocence* bears the date 1789, and it is likely that, satisfied with his new method, Blake in a hopeful mood began work on the title-page of his next book of poems.

A contemporary account by John Thomas Smith (1766–1833), a fellow engraver, tells of visionary aid. When Blake's brother Robert had died in 1787, Blake had seen his spirit rising 'through the matter-of-fact ceiling, "clapping his hands for joy"'. His brother's spirit continued to be present to him. After Blake 'had deeply perplexed himself as to the mode of accomplishing the publication of his illustrated songs, without their being subject to the expense of letter-press, his brother Robert stood before him in one of his visionary imaginations, and so decidedly directed him in the way in which he ought to proceed, that he immediately followed his advice, by writing his poetry, and drawing his marginal subjects of embellishments in outline upon the copper-plate with an impervious liquid, and then eating the plain parts or lights away with aqua fortis considerably below them, so that the outlines were left as a stereotype.'

30 *Songs of Innocence, c.* 1825. Frontispiece.

Ruthven Todd, with the help of the painter Joan Miró (1893–1983), experimented in the production of a reversed image of this kind. This is done by writing in the varnish on a sheet of paper, then reversing the paper on to the copper-plate, under pressure: a very delicate process.

Blake's watercolour illumination, carried out by hand, also owed something to supernatural inspiration. According to Gilchrist, 'He ground and mixed his watercolours himself on a piece of statuary marble, after a method of his own, with common carpenter's glue diluted, which he had found out, as the early Italians had before him, to be a good binder. Joseph, the sacred carpenter, had appeared in vision and revealed *that* secret to him.' Ruthven Todd thought that 'carpenter's glue' would have been too coarse and that some more refined substance was used. 'The colours he used were few and simple,' Gilchrist continues, 'indigo, cobalt, gamboge, vermilion, Frankfort-black freely, ultramarine rarely, chrome not at all. These he applied with a camel's hair brush, not with a sable which he disliked.'

Blake never printed off his two thousand copies, or made his fortune, but for the rest, Cumberland's letter foretold some of the advantages of the method. He could print copies as he needed them: he continued to print *Songs of Innocence*, and later *Songs of Innocence and of Experience*, from time to time to the end of his life, as he did his later books, whenever he found a purchaser. The inks he used were various: blue, green, bluish green, golden brown or black. Occasionally inks of two colours are combined in the same plate. But the unique character of each copy is created by the watercolour 'illumination'. There are great variations: each copy has its own colour-range and is a unique creation. Early copies of *Songs of Innocence* often have the transparency and delicacy of a rainbow, while some later copies are richly sombre, glowing with gold paint, like those medieval psalters which were doubtless Blake's inspiration.

Songs of Innocence comprises thirty-one plates in all, but their number and order varies in the twenty-three known copies of the book. 'The Little Girl Lost' and 'The Little Girl Found' were later transferred to *Songs of Experience*. As with others of his books – including *Milton* and *Jerusalem* – a final order was never absolutely determined.

The writing, engraving, printing and colouring – even the mixing of the pigments – was all Blake's work; the binding was done by his wife, who also learned to take off impressions from the plates. Some of the copies which have survived are also thought to be coloured with a rather heavy hand by Catherine.

Songs of Innocence may have been planned as a book for children, but once he was involved in its making, Blake soon lost sight of any purpose but the creation of beauty. However, *The Gates of Paradise*, a book of emblems engraved in 1793, is entitled *For Children*. At the end of the eighteenth century books for children were much in evidence, most of them, like Anna Laetitia Barbauld's *Hymns in Prose for Children* (1781) and Isaac Watts' *Divine and Moral Songs for Children*, first published in 1715, having a moral and religious character. Mary Wollstonecraft translated from the German Salzmann's *Elements of Morality for the Use of Parents and Children*, a book of simple incidents from real life, with a great number of illustrations, some of which were engraved by Blake. No doubt Mary's own *Original Stories from Real Life* (for which Blake drew ten and engraved five illustrations) was suggested by Salzmann's book. Mary Wollstonecraft (who worked as French editor for Blake's friend Johnson the bookseller) was under the influence of Rousseau, whose view of childhood as a law unto itself contrasted strongly with the pedagogic habit of mind in the Age of Reason. It must have been during his association with Mary that Blake formed the idea of making books for children, and about childhood, which should reflect the belief he shared with Rousseau that the unfolding of the imagination of every creature, in freedom, is the only true education.

26, 27   In *Tiriel*, a poem illustrated with drawings but not published, Blake had already denounced the current view of childhood – deriving in great measure from John Locke (1632–1704), that early forerunner of behaviourism and brain-washing – as a passive state to be 'formed' by 'instruction'. The poem describes with scathing indignation the consequences of 'forming' a child according to the laws of mechanistic rationalism, imposed all from outside and regardless of the mysterious formative laws of life itself. Tiriel, the blind parental tyrant, is himself the product of such an education, and dies cursing those who, by compelling him into conformity, had denied him life. For Rousseau, every child was unique; and Blake's

34   aphorism – illustrated, in *The Marriage of Heaven and Hell*, by Nebuchadnezzar compelled to eat grass – 'One Law for the Lion and Ox is Oppression' might summarize Rousseau's and Mary Wollstonecraft's views on education as well as his own. For 'Infancy', Rousseau wrote, 'has a manner of perceiving, thinking and feeling peculiar to itself.' Premature instruction is 'without regard to the peculiar genius of each. For, besides the constitution common to its species, each child at its birth possesses a peculiar temperament, which determines its genius and character; and which it is improper either to pervert or

The Blossom.

Merry Merry Sparrow
Under leaves so green
A happy Blossom
Sees you swift as arrow
Seek your cradle narrow
Near my Bosom.

Pretty Pretty Robin
Under leaves so green
A happy Blossom
Hears you sobbing sobbing
Pretty Pretty Robin
Near my Bosom.

31 *Songs of Innocence,* c. 1825. 'The Blossom.'

32 *Songs of Innocence,* c. 1825. 'The Ecchoing Green.'

restrain, the business of education being only to model and bring it to perfection. All the vices imputed to malignity of disposition are only the effect of the bad form it has received... there is not a villain upon earth, whose natural propensity, well directed, might not have been productive of great virtues.'

So also thought Blake, who many years later said that he had never known a bad man who had not something very good about him. Blake's realization that 'Every man's genius is peculiar to his individuality' is one he shared with Rousseau and Mary Wollstonecraft.

Blake was also a Platonist; he attacked Locke in his first engraved aphorisms, *There is no Natural Religion*, precisely for his refusal to accept Plato's view that there are innate ideas. 'Knowledge of Ideal Beauty is Not to be Acquired. It is Born with us. Innate Ideas are in Every Man. Born with him; they are truly Himself,' wrote Blake in about 1808 in the margins of Reynolds' *Discourses on Painting*; and again, in his old age, he wrote in the margin of his copy of Berkeley's *Siris* (1744): 'the Spiritual Body or Angel as little Children always behold the Face of the Heavenly Father'.

This, of course, goes beyond Rousseau – beyond Plato, indeed. For the essence of Blake's Christianity was his vision of the 'God within', 'Jesus the Imagination'. Childhood, for Blake, is the purest essence of the spirit of life; the thing itself. The instructions of education can add nothing to Being. 'Everything that lives is holy', not by virtue of any added qualities, but in its essence:

'I have no name,
'I am but two days old.'
What shall I call thee?
'I happy am,
'Joy is my name.'

Blake in these seemingly naïve lines is describing the nature of life as he conceived it. Joy – delight – is the essence of life, and all life seeks joy as its natural state. For him, the mechanistic view of the universe – the popular mentality of the Enlightenment under the guise of Deism ('natural religion'), the philosophy of Bacon, Newton and Locke – was the enemy of life; life which is immeasurable, not to be captured or contained within the quantitative 'laws of nature' – a view which Henri Bergson (1859–1941) was later to develop in more strictly philosophic terms.

'The hours of folly are measured by the clock; but the hours of wisdom no clock can measure.' As against the Newtonian universe, overwhelming man's sense of his own value by awe-inspiring vistas of space and time, Blake affirmed the holiness of life, omnipresent, no less in the tiny than in the vast:

To see a World in a Grain of Sand,
And heaven in a Wild Flower,
Hold Infinity in the palm of your hand
And Eternity in an hour.

All Blake's most characteristic and beautiful images are of the minute: the wild thyme and the meadowsweet – 'And none can tell how from so small a centre comes such sweets.' 'The little winged fly', the worm, the ant, the grasshopper and spider; the little bird – lark or nightingale or robin redbreast; the 'moment in each day that Satan cannot find' in which the poet's work is done; and, above all, the supreme symbol of the *multum in parvule*, the Divine Child. Life is neither great nor small, and the dignity of every living essence is not relative but absolute. Childhood – innocence – was for him not a state of inexperience and ignorance, but the state of pure being.

In *Songs of Innocence* the energy and spontaneity of life runs through every line of Blake's leaping, running, flying figures, the tendrils of his 'wandering vine', symbol of the one life in all things, which is, in the world of Innocence, not a theory but a state of being. Simple as these poems may be in form, they contain a great wisdom and rest upon the firm ground of philosophy. They embody essential knowledge more enduring than the imposing structures of conceptual thought elaborated by the philosophers of the Enlightenment and their French counterparts, Voltaire, Diderot and the Encyclopedists. This is no less a miracle of imaginative insight for the fact that Blake was deeply and widely read, not only in the works of those whom he attacked, but also in the writings of mystics and philosophers such as Plato and Plotinus, George Berkeley and the *Hermetica*, Paracelsus and Robert Fludd, and the mystical theology of Jakob Boehme and Emanuel Swedenborg.

The apparent weightlessness of Blake's figures, the ease with which they fly without the use of those cumbrous wings Baroque, and still more, Victorian angels required, arises from the realization that life, as Blake understood it, is not subject to the forces of nature. Life – consciousness – moves freely where it wills. To leap in thought along the line of a hill, or on to a cloud, is to be there in imagination.

Already in *Songs of Innocence* Blake's figures have attained freedom from the gravitational forces which constrain material objects: the characteristic, thereafter, of all his depictions of the human form, a quality essentially Blakean, and shared by none of his contemporaries. Again, he may have been influenced in this by Early Christian art, and those angels and heavenly personages who are essentially, and not merely in name, immaterial beings occupying mental and not physical space.

In the five years between *Songs of Innocence* and *Songs of Experience* Blake produced two illuminated books of outstanding beauty: *The Book of Thel* (1789) and *The Marriage of Heaven and Hell* (1790–3). *Thel* is close in spirit to the paradisal world of *Songs of Innocence*. It consists of seven engraved plates, about six inches by four and a quarter; the larger size suggests that Blake was now more confident about his technique. The designs express, even more than those of *Songs of Innocence*, the easy grace, freedom and expressive sweetness characteristic of Blake's vision of 'Innocence'. The 'fair luminous mist' of the colour-washes Blake now began to use over the whole page seems to illuminate words and designs alike with the light of Paradise. The theme of the poem is Neoplatonic, and draws much upon Thomas Taylor's recently published paraphrased translation of Plotinus' *On the Beautiful*, and on the idea of the 'descent' of the soul into generation as described in this and other works of Taylor which appeared about this time.

The Marriage of Heaven and Hell, engraved about a year later, reflects in its fiery forms and colours the ideas of 'Hell, or Energy', no less characteristic of Blake's thought. Before

28, 33

34–6,
38

33 *The Book of Thel*, 1789. 'Matron Clay.'

the Terror and the ensuing slaughter of so many of the early liberal supporters of the French Revolution – members of the Gironde, friends of Mary Wollstonecraft and of Thomas Paine (1737–1809) – Blake had worn the *bonnet rouge* in the streets of London. He was a Republican, and had hailed revolution first in America, then in France, as an expression of freedom, and of that spirit of life which was, for him, in whatever guise, holy. When in France the reality proved to be otherwise, Blake changed his mind about the value of political solutions. 'I am really sorry to see my Countrymen trouble themselves about Politics,' he wrote in about 1809, having seen twenty years of 'glorious revolution' and its ensuing wars. 'If Men were Wise, the Most arbitrary Princes could not hurt them; if they are not wise, the Freest Government is compell'd to be a Tyranny.' Politics seemed to him 'to be something Else besides Human Life'. He at all times hated war, believing that the arts could only flourish in peaceful States. 'Rome & Greece swept Art into their maw & destroy'd it; a Warlike State never can produce Art. It will Rob & Plunder & accumulate into one place, & Translate & Copy & Buy & Sell & Criticise, but not Make.' *Europe: A Prophecy* is an indictment of war written at a time when Blake and his friends hoped that England would not go to war with France; but later, in his 'apotheoses' of Pitt and Nelson (1809) it seems that Blake was a supporter of the national cause against Napoleon: if not in the conventional sense, at least in the prophetic region of spiritual causes. But the 'happy country' of which he called himself a citizen was the 'Kingdom not of this world'.

Meanwhile, in *The Marriage of Heaven and Hell* 'the newborn terror', Orc, the child who burns in the flames of his own energy, is hailed as the Messiah of the New Age whose prophet Blake believed himself to be. Of all Blake's books, this has perhaps the greatest power of word and of design. The literary form is no longer lyric, but aphorism and parable of visionary events experienced 'behind the veil'. 'Energy is eternal delight'; and life – no less holy in 'the new-born terror' of 'the fiery limbs, the flaming hair' than in the unhampered child on its cloud in *Songs of Innocence* – obeys the law of its innate energies. Free, life is mild and loving; impeded, it is rebellious and violent. Energy enchained, like Nebuchadnezzar, whose royal humanity was compelled into the grass-eating nature of the 'patient ox', becomes warlike and fierce. All Blake's sympathies, in this book, are with lion and devil, giant and fiery serpent of 'the nether deep'. His tyrants are kings, churches, parents, schoolmasters. 'The tygers of wrath are wiser than the horses of instruction.'

No doubt this book is an expression of Blake's mood of sympathy with the forces of revolution, seen as an expression of the irrepressible energy of life. But it is, at the same time, the fruit of his profound studies of the mystical theology of Boehme, the alchemical writings of Paracelsus, Fludd and Agrippa, and his knowledge of the Western Esoteric tradition both orthodox and heterodox. Christianity, in its popular forms at all events, has never sufficiently understood what Carl Jung (1875–1961) called the ambivalence of the archetypes. No psychic energy, or mood of the soul, is merely good or merely evil; the face turned depends upon circumstances. This is a truth well understood in Mahayana Buddhism, whose deities have their peaceful and angry aspects; and also in Hinduism, where Kali and Shiva have their mild and their terrible faces; or in the ancient Greek religion; or in the Jewish mystical tradition of the Cabbalistic Tree of the Sephiroth. Jakob Boehme (1575–1624), perhaps more profoundly than any other Christian mystic, had understood this truth, and Blake followed him. Far beyond merely 'religious' thought, the *Marriage* is a work of prophetic vision into the nature of vital causes; 'inspired' in the sense in which we use the word of the Hebrew prophets, as Blake himself claimed. It is the 'Poetic Genius', Blake declared, that spoke through the prophets Isaiah and Ezekiel, of whom all the 'gods' of the Gentiles are tributaries; 'it was this that our great poet, King David, desired so fervently & invokes so pathetic'ly, saying by this he conquers enemies & governs kingdoms'. And here Blake's 'Jesus, the Imagination' appears for the first time in opposition to Milton's 'Messiah, or Reason': 'in the Book of Job, Milton's Messiah is call'd Satan'. Jesus, Blake concludes, 'was all virtue, and acted from impulse, not from rules'. The premiss is the same as that of *Songs of Innocence*, but more bold in its extension.

Because Blake wrote in *The Marriage of Heaven and Hell* that 'Without Contraries is no progression', it has often been assumed that the states of Innocence and Experience represent a pair of contraries like his Reason and Energy, or the peace of Heaven and the 'fires of genius'. This is not so, for 'a negation is not a contrary', he says. The state of Innocence was not, for Blake, one of ignorance, as compared with the wisdom of 'experience' so highly valued by Voltaire's Candide or Dr Johnson's Rasselas, types of the Enlightenment. The state of Innocence is that of unclouded, unhindered life; and as Blake's symbol of that state is the child, so 'aged ignorance', clipping the wings of youth, is his symbol of Experience. The title-page of *Experience* shows two weepers by a 'gothic' tomb, where the 'dead' – the spiritually dead – lie like effigies on their own tombs. Blake's 'Hell, or Energy' is one of the modes of life; 'the

37

40

pulse, not from rules.

When he had so spoken: I beheld the Angel who
stretched out his arms embracing the flame of fire
& he was consumed, and arose as Elijah

Note. This Angel, who is now become a Devil, is
my particular friend: we often read the Bible to-
-gether in its infernal or diabolical sense which
the world shall have if they behave well

I have also: The Bible of Hell: which the world
shall have whether they will or no.

One Law for the Lion & Ox is Oppression

roaring of lions, the howling of wolves, the raging of the stormy sea, and the destructive sword, are portions of eternity, too great for the eye of man'. Experience is the antithesis of life. Life may be impeded and denied: by unrequited love as in 'The Angel' or 'Ah! Sunflower'; by childhood oppressed, as in 'Nurse's Song' and 'The Chimney Sweeper'; by moral oppression as in 'The Garden of Love' and 'A Little Girl Lost'; or by social injustice, as in 'London'. The 'net of religion' spread by 'aged ignorance' runs through all; and the dark face of the human city evoked in 'London' is but the sum of inhumanity and of the perversion and restraint of life for which every individual is in some measure responsible:

In every cry of every Man,
In every Infant's cry of fear,
In every voice, in every ban,
The mind-forg'd manacles I hear.

34 OPPOSITE ABOVE *The Marriage of Heaven and Hell*, c. 1794. 'Nebuchadnezzar.'
35 OPPOSITE BELOW *The Marriage of Heaven and Hell*, c. 1794. Title-page. In the lower part an Angel in clouds and a Devil in flames embrace. Above is the surface of the earth.
36 ABOVE *The Marriage of Heaven and Hell*, c. 1796. 'The soul hovering over the body.'

The Giants who formed this world into its
sensual existence and now seem to live in it
in chains are in truth, the causes of its life
& the sources of all activity, but the chains
are, the cunning of weak and tame minds, which
have power to resist energy, according to the pro
verb, the weak in courage is strong in cunning.
Thus one portion of being, is the Prolific, the
other, the Devouring; to the devourer it seems as
if the producer was in his chains, but it is not so,
he only takes portions of existence and fancies
that the whole. ―― ―――
But the Prolific would cease to be Prolific
unless the Devourer as a sea recieved the excess
of his delights. ――
Some will say, Is not God alone the Prolific?
I answer. God only Acts & Is, in existing beings
or Men. ――
These two classes of men are always upon
earth. & they should be enemies; whoever tries

37 ABOVE LEFT *The Gates of Paradise*, 1793. 'Aged Ignorance'. Perceptive Organs
closed, their Objects close.
38 ABOVE RIGHT *The Marriage of Heaven and Hell, c.* 1794. 'Ugolino and his sons
in prison.'
39 OPPOSITE *Songs of Innocence and of Experience*, 1794. Frontispiece.

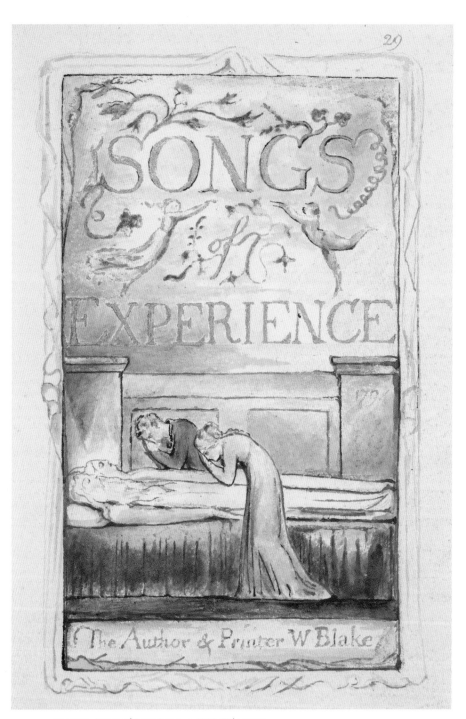

40 ABOVE *Songs of Experience, c.* 1825. Title-page.
41 OPPOSITE ABOVE *Songs of Experience, c.* 1825. 'The Sick Rose.'
42 OPPOSITE BELOW *Songs of Experience, c.* 1825. 'London.'

The Tyger.

Tyger Tyger. burning bright,
In the forests of the night;
What immortal hand or eye,
Could frame thy fearful symmetry?

In what distant deeps or skies,
Burnt the fire of thine eyes?
On what wings dare he aspire?
What the hand, dare sieze the fire?

And what shoulder, & what art,
Could twist the sinews of thy heart?
And when thy heart began to beat,
What dread hand? & what dread feet?

What the hammer? what the chain,
In what furnace was thy brain?
What the anvil? what dread grasp,
Dare its deadly terrors clasp?

When the stars threw down their spears.
And water'd heaven with their tears:
Did he smile his work to see?
Did he who made the Lamb make thee?

Tyger Tyger burning bright,
In the forests of the night:
What immortal hand or eye,
Dare frame thy fearful symmetry?

It is these 'mind-forg'd manacles' (sometimes depicted as shackling the feet of Urizen, the false god) which make thorns where there should be roses, furtive 'whisperings' instead of childish laughter, 'tombstones where flowers should be'. Blake indicts Church and State, parents, nurses and schoolmasters; but also, and above all, the tortuousness of 'the Human Brain', whose reasonings confound the simplicity of life, and which 'knits a snare' in which souls become inextricably entangled, as in a spider's web of prohibitions and hypocrisy. Many of the poems of *Experience* are antithetical to those of *Innocence*; the difference between 'Infant Sorrow' and 'Infant Joy' is that between love and the absence of love. The 'Ecchoing Green' is a childhood world surrounded by sympathy, 'Nurse's Song' is childhood clouded by the sick thoughts of the Nurse: an anticipation of Henry James's *Turn of the Screw*. The 'Holy Thursday' of *Experience* is an indictment of cold charity; the poverty of the children is above all in the absence of love:

And their sun does never shine,
And their fields are bleak & bare,
And their ways are fill'd with thorns:
It is eternal winter there.

'The Chimney Sweeper' of *Innocence* can escape in dreams into a heavenly country; but *Experience* reminds us that the crimes of society against the children of the poor are none the less for that. Nor is it only the poor who are oppressed, but the schoolboy, forced to the joyless routine of learning; or 'A Little Boy Lost' oppressed by the Calvinist morality which immolates souls if no longer bodies.

The figures of *Experience* are entangled, burdened, listless or dead. A burning jewel in that sombre setting is 'The Tyger'. In this great poem, as in 'To Tirzah' (added about 1801), we again find Blake seeking to rend the veil and to bring to light the meaning and the mystery of evil. In 'To Tirzah' we find, as in *Thel*, the Neoplatonic view of 'mortal birth' as itself the greatest of evils. In 'The Tyger' there are traces of the *Hermetica*, of the mystical theology of Boehme, of the esoteric philosophy of alchemy. But the poem ends with the question unanswered: 'Did he who made the Lamb, make thee?'

43

43 *Songs of Experience*, 1794. 'The Tyger.'

Chapter 4
'Lovely Lambeth'

Blake had left Poland Street in 1790, soon after the death of his mother, from which we may surmise that it was his affection for her that had kept him in the neighbourhood of his family. Blake is said to have spoken little of his parents later in life – only of his brother Robert. Blake and Catherine now moved to 13 Hercules Buildings, Lambeth, on the south bank of the Thames. Gilchrist describes the house as a humble one-storeyed building; but Frederick Tatham (1805–78), an artist friend of Blake's later years, remembers it as 'a pretty, clean house of eight or ten rooms', a typical London terrace house of the eighteenth century, with the usual strip of garden behind. In this garden grew a 'wandering vine', unpruned, to form the arbour where, according to one of those legends which no official denial can kill, Mr and Mrs Blake were once surprised by a friend in the dress of Eden, with the addition only of helmets (a detail which comes through the painter George Richmond), occupied in the reading aloud of *Paradise Lost*.

The seven years at Lambeth were both productive and happy; the Lambeth Books include all Blake's finest illuminated books with the exception of *Milton* and *Jerusalem*. In *Jerusalem*, most of which was written in South Molton Street, the poet recalls 'Lovely Lambeth':

There the secret furniture of Jerusalem's chamber
Is wrought. Lambeth! The Bride, the Lamb's Wife, loveth thee.
Thou art one with her & knowest not of Self in Thy supreme joy.
Go on, builders in hope, tho' Jerusalem wanders far away.

And again:

There is a Grain of Sand in Lambeth that Satan cannot find,

> Nor can his Watch Fiends find it; 'tis translucent & has many
>   Angles,
> But he who finds it will find Oothoon's palace; for within
> Opening into Beulah, every angle is a lovely heaven.
> But should the Watch Fiends find it, they would call it Sin.

Beulah, in Blake's symbolic language, represents the married
state. The second of these passages thus suggests that Lambeth
was a place and time not only of happy toil but of happy love.

But if this was a creative and, it seems, a happy time in
Blake's life, the Lambeth Books are the most turbulent, sombre
and pessimistic of all his writings. Blake is less persuasive
when he speaks with the voice of revolutionary violence than
when he works in the clear light of the vision of eternity.
Perhaps he was trying to persuade himself that the political
violence of the time was a short cut to spiritual liberation;
or it may be simply that the clouds and thunders of the age
are reflected in his poetry and designs: 'In troubled mists,
o'erclouded by the terrors of struggling times.'

44-8   In 1793 Blake engraved and published *The Gates of Paradise*,
a little book of emblems with seventeen plates, each one of
them unforgettable. Their theme is Job's question, engraved on
the frontispiece: 'What is Man?' Blake's answer is indicated by
the symbol of metamorphosis. A caterpillar, symbol of 'natural
man', consumes the leaf of our native Druid tree, the oak; and
on another leaf, an infant sleeping in a chrysalis signifies the
'second birth' of the 'spiritual body' of humanity, latent in
the human animal. It was the Jews' discovery and exploration
of that new Kingdom of the Human, the revelation of its laws,
the living of life in accordance with the 'divine humanity',
the 'Imagination', that, for Blake, entitled them to their title
of a 'chosen people'. 'We of Israel taught that the Poetic Genius
(as you now call it) was the first principle and all the others
merely derivative, which was the cause of our despising the
Priests & Philosophers of other countries, and prophecying
that all Gods would at last be proved to originate in ours &
to be the tributaries of the Poetic Genius.' For the emblem of
metamorphosis, however, Blake was indebted to the Greeks.

The four Michelangelesque figures of Earth, Air, Fire
and Water anticipate those Four Zoas whose mythological
adventures form the substance of the Prophetic Books which
were to follow. The number four, as Jung pointed out, is by
no means arbitrary, but corresponds to the four functions, or
energies, of the psyche; the 'four living creatures' of the Book
of Ezekiel and the Apocalypse of St John. To these Biblical
theriomorphic forms (i.e. deities depicted in animal form)

44, 45 TOP *The Gates of Paradise,* 1793. 'Water': 'Thou waterest him with Tears'; and 'Earth': 'He struggles into Life'.
46 ABOVE *The Gates of Paradise,* 1793. 'I have said to the Worm: Thou art my mother and my sister'.
47, 48 OPPOSITE *The Gates of Paradise,* 1793. 'Air': 'On Cloudy Doubts of Reasoning Cares'; 'Fire': 'That end in endless Strife'.

Air

Published 17 May 1793 by W Blake Lambeth

4

Fire

Pub.d by W Blake 17 May 1793

5

Blake was to give human attributes and features that are unforgettable. The Four Zoas seem likely to become figures as familiar in our national mythology as Hamlet and Lear.

Some of these mythological figures are already discernible in the *Songs*. Chief among them is the figure of the soul, or psyche (the *anima*, in Jung's terminology). As 'The Little Girl Lost' she clearly has an affinity with the Kore of the Eleusinian Mysteries. She reappears as the gentle Thel, reluctant to 'descend' into the Underworld of Generation; and in *Visions of the Daughters of Albion* (1793) she becomes Oothoon, who, more heroic than Thel, makes the 'descent' and suffers. In later works (1795–1804) she is Vala, and in the poem which originally bore her name (afterwards entitled *The Four Zoas*), she re-enacts the Latin novelist Apuleius' (b. 125) legend of Cupid and Psyche. Her final form (1804–20) is as Jerusalem, the Bride of the Lamb. There is a deepening and development of the figure, but the story is essentially the same in all the versions. The soul 'descends' into the cave, or grave, of this world; willingly in the case of Lyca ('The Little Girl Lost'), reluctantly in the case of Thel. In both these poems it is implied that the soul has a task to perform in the World of Generation. In *Visions of the Daughters of Albion* we see her, as Oothoon, bitterly lamenting, like Debussy's Melisande, and protesting that on earth the laws are not those of the spirit. This poem is Blake's indictment of the cruelty of the sexual morality of the world. The unmarried are driven into sorrowful fantasies, and for woman, indissoluble marriage is an enslavement to lust when law and not love is the bond. Blake was surely thinking of his friend Mary Wollstonecraft and her heroic protest on behalf of women, leading to her own tragedy and early death. The poem contains some magnificent passages of poetry, developing Blake's conception of every creature as a unique expression of ever-various life. The law each creature must obey is innate; therefore 'one Law for the Lion & Ox is Oppression'.

On the title-page of *Visions of the Daughters of Albion* appears the figure later named Urizen: the blind tyrant, 'aged ignorance', the rational law-giver, in pursuit of the soul of life. Under the tyranny of Blake's grey-bearded Prince of this World, a travesty of God the Father, whose laws are imposed upon the energies of life that is its own law, Oothoon is bound to Bromion, her ravisher, by the fetters of legality. Her lover, Theotormon, unable to see that the soul is in its essence incorruptible (a Plotinian rather than a Christian doctrine), 'converses with shadows dire'.

Blake's depiction of Urizen advancing with outspread arms and vast beard derives, as mentioned earlier, from a Roman sculpture of Jupiter Pluvius. The same figure had appeared

49

50

49 *Visions of the Daughters of Albion,* 1793. Frontispiece: Oothoon and Bromion tied back to back in a cave, while Theotormon mourns.

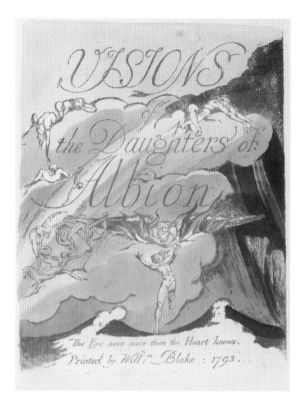

50 *Visions of the Daughters of Albion,* 1793. Title-page.

in an engraving made by Blake in 1791 for his friend Fuseli, as an illustration for Erasmus Darwin's *Botanic Garden,* where it represented the advancing flood of the Nile. This figure gradually developed – in *The First Book of Urizen* (1794) especially – the familiar features of Blake's unhappy, blind, self-deluded world-ruler: not God but misguided human reason. This is one among a number of such visual sources common to Blake, Flaxman, Fuseli and others of their circle.

The figure of Urizen is already present in *Songs of Experience* (1789–94), entangled in the 'net of religion'; he is 'starry jealousy' of 'Earth's Answer', the 'Jealous God' of Puritanism:

Selfish father of men!
Cruel, jealous, selfish fear!
Can delight,
Chain'd in night,
The virgins of youth and morning bear?

In *The Marriage of Heaven and Hell* (1790–3) he is 'the starry king' who is overcome by the fiery child, later developed as

'Red Orc', spirit of the energy of life. Orc is Eros, but he is also violence and revolution; for 'When Thought is closed in Caves Then love will shew its root in deepest Hell.'

Like the gods of any ancient mythology, the Zoas, in their acts, attributes and appearances, have an archetypal quality to which we respond, not as to a work of art, but as to the spiritual realities themselves, as if these had existence in their own right. We recognize in them the images of gods in the world of modern industrial England; they are not figments of Blake's personal fantasy, but embodiments of the moods and energies of the collective life of the nation. They are ourselves.

51-6 In *America* (1793), we find Blake's natural mythological genius uneasily harnessed to a specific political theme – the American War of Independence, which is treated in the same manner as *The French Revolution.* Nothing more effectively ensures the obscurity of poetry to later generations than those very topical allusions which are at the time as clear as the headlines in a daily paper and as soon forgotten. Figures of the day – Washington, Franklin, Paine, Warren, Gates, Hancock and Green – 'show', in Gilchrist's words, 'small and remote, perplexed and busied in an ant-like way'; while Orc, 'the Shadowy Female', and Urizen live on with a fierce and turbulent life into our own world. Several of the plates are very fine.

Blake's admirers are divided into those who see him as a political propagandist who regrettably strayed away from direct engagement in the issues of his day into incomprehensible mysticism; and those for whom he was a mystic and visionary who discerned, as did the Hebrew Prophets, the spiritual causes behind history. For the scholars David Erdman (1911–2001) and Jacob Bronowski (1908–74), Blake's prophetic allegories were a disguise he was forced to adopt by the danger of speaking openly on political issues at the time of the French Revolution (especially after Britain had declared war on France). To others, Blake's spiritual vision seems clearer than his politics. Blake was not at any time thinking on the same plane as Paine or William Godwin (1756–1836); like Shelley (who may possibly have seen some of Blake's Prophetic Books at Godwin's house), he saw the warfare in 'heaven' – that is, the inner worlds – in whose engagement the mortal actors are mere puppets in some great drama of the collective consciousness.

For Blake, outward events and circumstances were the *expressions* of states of mind, ideologies, mentalities, and not, as for the determinist-materialist ideologies of the modern world, their causes. Blake's 'dark Satanic Mills', so often invoked in the name of social reform, prove, when we read *Milton* (the poem in which these mills are most fully described)

51 ABOVE LEFT *America: A Prophecy*,
1793. Orc in the fires of energy.
For Blake, 'War is energy enslav'd'.
52 ABOVE RIGHT *America: A Prophecy*,
1793. Title-page.
53 LEFT *America: A Prophecy*, 1793.
Frontispiece.
54 OPPOSITE ABOVE *America:
A Prophecy*, 1793. Orc fettered by
Los and Enitharmon (time and space).
55 OPPOSITE BELOW *America:
A Prophecy*, 1793. Orc: 'The hairy
shoulders rend the links'.

The shadowy daughter of Urthona stood before red Orc.
When fourteen suns had faintly journey'd o'er his dark abode;
His food she brought in iron baskets, his drink in cups of iron;
Crown'd with a helmet & dark hair the nameless female stood;
A quiver with its burning stores, a bow like that of night,
When pestilence is shot from heaven; no other arms she need:
Invulnerable tho' naked, save where clouds roll round her loins,
Their awful folds in the dark air; silent she stood as night;
For never from her iron tongue could voice or sound arise;
But dumb till that dread day when Orc assay'd his fierce embrace.

Dark virgin; said the hairy youth, thy father stern abhorr'd;
Rivets my tenfold chains while still on high my spirit soars;
Sometimes an eagle screaming in the sky, sometimes a lion,
Stalking upon the mountains, & sometimes a whale I lash
The raging fathomless abyss, anon a serpent folding
Around the pillars of Urthona, and round thy dark limbs,
On the Canadian wilds I fold, feeble my spirit folds,
For chaind beneath I rend these caverns; when thou bringest food
I howl my joy, and my red eyes seek to behold thy face,
In vain! these clouds roll to & fro, & hide thee from my sight.

Silent as despairing love, and strong as jealousy,
The hairy shoulders rend the links, free are the wrists of fire;
Round the terrific loins he siez'd the panting, struggling, womb;
It joy'd: she put aside her clouds & smiled her first-born smile;
As when a black cloud shews its lightnings to the silent deep.

Soon as she saw the terrible boy then burst the virgin cry.

I know thee, I have found thee, & I will not let thee go;
Thou art the image of God who dwells in darkness of Africa;
And thou art fall'n to give me life in regions of dark death.
On my American plains I feel the struggling afflictions
Endur'd by roots that writhe their arms into the nether deep:
I see a serpent in Canada, who courts me to his love;
In Mexico an Eagle, and a Lion in Peru;
I see a Whale in the South-sea, drinking my soul away.
O what limb rending pains I feel, thy fire & my frost
Mingle in howling pains, in furrows by thy lightnings rent;
This is eternal death; and this the torment long foretold.

56 *America: A Prophecy,* c. 1794–6. Cancelled plate: 'A Dream of Thiralatha'.

to be the mechanistic 'laws' of Bacon, Newton and Locke, of which the industrial landscape was a reflection and expression. Man has made his machines in the image of his ideology. So, always, Blake seeks to discover the source of social and private ills within man. Only a change of the heart and mind of the nation can create a new society and new cities less hideous than those created by an atheist and mechanistic rationalism.

Blake gradually renounced politics for something more radical: not religion, in the sense of a system of beliefs and observances, but a transformation of the inner life, a rebirth of 'the true man'. Politics and religion alike came to seem to him an evasion of the 'one thing needful'.

This is not to say that Blake's 'prophetic' poems no longer related to current history; rather, he saw history from within; in the succession to the Prophets of Israel, he addressed the English nation at the level of spiritual causes, not of day-to-day policy. 'Every Natural Effect has a Spiritual Cause Not a Natural; for a Natural cause only seems.'

57-60 His *Europe: A Prophecy* followed *America* a year later, in 1794. It contains seventeen quarto pages, among them some of the
61 most beautiful Blake ever made. The frontispiece, *The Ancient of Days*, published also as a separate plate, bears little relation to the theme of the poem, which describes the fiery activities of 'Red Orc' trampling the grapes of wrath in the 'vineyards' of France. *The Bellman, The Plague,* and the companion plates *War* and *Famine* are more topical and illustrate the horrors of war. The more decorative designs include one of the gayest of Blake's depictions of the untrammelled energies of life: two 'spiritual bodies or angels', or perhaps fairies, blowing flower-like trumpets as they speed through a minute world of grass-blades and ears of barley. Tendrils endowed with the energy of serpents advance to meet lines of verse much inferior to the accompanying designs.

62-6 The title of *The First Book of Urizen*, also of 1794 (there was never a 'second' Book of Urizen), suggests on the analogy of the 'first' and 'second' Books of Kings, Samuel, etc. that it belonged to Blake's 'Bible of Hell', promised to the world in *The Marriage*

57 *Europe: A Prophecy,* 1794. Mildew blighting ears of corn.

And the clouds & fires pale rolld round in the night of Enitharmon
Round Albions cliffs & Londons walls: still Enitharmon slept:
Rolling volumes of grey mist involve Churches, Palaces, Towers:
For Urizen unclaspd his Book: feeding his soul with pity
The youth of England hid in gloom curse the pained heavens; compelld
Into the deadly night to see the form of Albions Angel
Their parents brought them forth & left them in ignorance prophecy ranting.
In a vast rock, perceivd by those senses that are closd from thought:
Bleak, dark, abrupt, it stands & overshadows London city
They saw his bony feet on the rock, the flesh consumd in flames:
They saw the Serpent temple lifted above, shadowing the Island white:
They heard the voice of Albions Angel howling in flames of Orc,
Seeking the trump of the last doom.

Above the rest the howl was heard from Westminster louder & louder:
The Guardian of the secret codes forsook his ancient mansion,
Driven out by the flames of Orc; his furrd robes & false locks
Adhered and grew one with his flesh, and nerves & veins shot thro them
With dismal torment sick hanging upon the wind: he fled
Groveling along Great George Street thro the Park gate: all the soldiers
Fled from his sight: he dragd his torments to the wilderness.

Thus was the howl thro Europe!
For Orc rejoicd to hear the howling shadows
But Palamabron shot his lightnings trenching down his wide back
And Rintrah hung with all his legions in the nether deep

Enitharmon laughd in her sleep to see (O womans triumph)
Every house a den, every man bound; the shadows are filld
With spectres, and the windows wove over with curses of iron:
Over the doors Thou shalt not; & over the chimneys Fear is written:
With bands of iron round their necks fastend into the walls
The citizens: in leaden gyves the inhabitants of suburbs
Walk heavy: soft and bent are the bones of villagers

Between the clouds of Urizen the flames of Orc roll heavy
Round the limbs of Albions Guardian, his flesh consuming.
Howlings & hissings, shrieks & groans, & voices of despair
Arise around him in the cloudy
Heavens of Albion, Furious

Now comes the night of Enitharmons joy!
Who shall I call? Who shall I send?
That Woman, lovely Woman! may have dominion?
Arise O Rintrah thee I call! & Palamabron thee!
Go! tell the human race that Womans love is Sin:
That an Eternal life awaits the worms of sixty winters
In an allegorical abode where existence hath never come:
Forbid all joy, & from her childhood shall the little female
Spread nets in every secret path.
My weary eyelids draw towards the evening, my bliss is yet but new.
                                                                      Arise

Albions Angel rose upon the Stone of Night.
He saw Urizen on the Atlantic:
And his brazen Book,
That Kings & Priests had copied on Earth
Expanded from North to South.

of Heaven and Hell. In this cosmological picture book, Blake deserts politics to depict and describe his tyrant demon Urizen. Some of the most effective plates have no text: as Gilchrist says, 'the volume seems to be a carefully finished selection of compositions from his portfolios and engraved books'. It was for this work that Blake first used an admixture of glue and paint as a colour-printing medium. The poem itself is a sombre satire of Milton's account of the Creation; according to Blake, the Seven Days of Creation represent seven phases of the imprisonment and 'binding' of 'the caverned man' within the limitations of a world experienced only through the five senses. Urizen, thus limited, becomes the self-deluded and anxious demiurge, engaged in the 'enormous labours' of imposing his 'ratio of the five senses' on rebellious life, whose nature he has not understood. Such, according to Blake, is 'human reason', the false God of the Enlightenment, and, in France, of Rousseau and Voltaire.

There are terrible and powerful depictions of constricted and distorted forms of life, suffering under the tyranny of Urizen's 'laws of nature' and a morality based upon natural, not spiritual, law. Spirits of life are drawn down from the region of consciousness which is, for every soul, its own place, into the dizzying abyss of time and space, Newton's 'soul-shuddering vacuum' – in terms of life, 'outside existence'. Into this realm of tyranny is born Orc, the Burning Babe, the spirit of life destined everywhere and always to defy the systematization of the rationalist.

With *The Song of Los*, *The Book of Ahania* and *The Book of Los* (all dated 1795) Blake seems to have exhausted the vein of his 'Bible of Hell'. In these later books other figures of his pantheon emerge: Los, spirit of time and of prophecy, and his consort Enitharmon (who is at once space, and the mother of those forms in which the imaginings of the artist are embodied). These figures were named (though scarcely realized, and not depicted) in *Europe* (1794). In *The First Book of Urizen* Los is the reluctant agent of the 'binding' of Urizen, and is himself 'rent apart' when Urizen is separated from the wholeness of humanity. Separated likewise from Enitharmon by this fall of man into division, he begets upon her the child Orc, who is (as in the archaic Greek pantheon, where each succeeding generation of gods overthrows the heaven-ruler) destined to overcome Urizen.

---

58 OPPOSITE ABOVE LEFT *Europe: A Prophecy*, 1794. Plate 14: 'And the clouds & fires...'.
59 OPPOSITE ABOVE RIGHT *Europe: A Prophecy*, 1794. Plate 7: 'Now comes the night...'.
60 OPPOSITE BELOW *Europe: A Prophecy*, 1794. Plate 12: 'Albions Angel rose...'.

61 ABOVE *The Ancient of Days*, 1794. Frontispiece from *Europe: A Prophecy*. 'When he sets a compass upon the face of the deep' (Proverbs 8: 27).
62 OPPOSITE ABOVE LEFT *The First Book of Urizen*, 1794. Immortals falling into the abyss of time and space created by the materialist philosophy of Bacon, Newton and Locke.
63 OPPOSITE ABOVE RIGHT *The First Book of Urizen*, 1794. Plate 21.

Urizen CH.III.

As the stars are apart from the earth
9. Los wept howling around the dark
Daman:
And cursing his lot for an anguish
Urizen was rent from his side
To a fathomless void for his feet
And intense fires for his dwelling

10. But Urizen laid in a stony sleep
Unorganized, rent from Eternity

11. The Eternals said: What is this Death
Urizen is a clod of clay

64 ABOVE LEFT *The First Book of Urizen,*
1794. Plate 18.
65 RIGHT *The First Book of Urizen,*
1794. Plate 16.

66 ABOVE *The First Book of Urizen*, 1794. Urizen struggling in the waters of materialism.
67 OPPOSITE Page from the *Vala* manuscript, 1797.

In *The Four Zoas* (1795–1804), *Milton* (1804–8) and *Jerusalem* (1804–20), Los and Enitharmon are more fully realized, and – with Blake's progressive loss of faith in revolution – Orc, spirit of revolution, recedes into the background. Urizen, still retaining the venerable features of 'aged ignorance', becomes the Satan of *Milton*. He makes his last, terrible appearance as the cloven-footed false image of God, who, in the *Illustrations of the Book of Job*, torments Job with his pretence to being the supreme God. Throughout Blake's work, the true world-ruler is 'Jesus, the Imagination', the 'God within', whose mystical marriage with the soul is celebrated in the last plate of *Jerusalem*.

Probably much of the *Vala* manuscript (later called *The Four Zoas*) was written in Lambeth. The poem is a palimpsest; additions, insertions and deletions were built round an earlier *Vala* poem, probably begun in 1791. *The Four Zoas* in its relatively final form represents a new beginning, incorporating portions of the earlier manuscript, which itself represents more than one attempt. There are a few striking pencil drawings – some of them so 'strange' that Tatham (to whom Catherine bequeathed Blake's papers) tried to rub them out; but the poem was never engraved or made into an illuminated book.

The interest of the manuscript is mainly literary. A beautiful passage in Night the Ninth retells, in a style reminiscent of *The Book of Thel* (1789), the story of Cupid and Psyche in terms of Blake's own pantheon, with Vala as the soul-figure, and Luvah (the 'eternal' form of Orc) as Eros. The poem contains some magnificent poetry; the passages spoken by Enion, the earth-mother, beginning 'What is the price of Experience?' (line 397 of Night the Second), and her speech at the end of Night the Seventh on resurrection of the 'eternal man', are unsurpassed in Blake's later works.

In this poem the Four Zoas and their Emanations – the pantheon of Blake's interior cosmos – take their final forms. Urizen and Orc remain, but the active agents of the soul's recovery from the 'sleep of death' are now the poetic genius (Los) and his 'Emanation', Enitharmon, who gives form to the imaginings of the 'Poetic Genius'. Two new figures – Enion and Tharmas – complete the 'fourfold' pattern of the psyche by the introduction of the mutable form, and formless energy, of the physical body.

Blake's poetic descriptions of the acts and attributes of these mythological beings are in themselves pictorial; we seem to know their appearance, behaviour, voices almost, as they existed in Blake's vivid visualizations.

During his seven years at Lambeth Blake produced, besides illuminated books, a number of designs. He had shown at the Royal Academy exhibition of 1785 four watercolour drawings: one from Gray, *The Bard*, the other three from the story of Joseph. A prospectus etched in 1793 advertises for sale 'at Mr Blake's, No. 13 Hercules Buildings, Lambeth', besides the illuminated books and *The Gates of Paradise*, 'Job, a Historical Engraving', 'Edward and Elinor, a Historical Engraving', and 'The History of England, a small book of Engravings'. Blake's first essay on the theme of *Job* illustrates the text which inspired *The Gates of Paradise*: 'What is man, that thou shouldst try him every Moment.' In the equally splendid companion print, on the death of Ezekiel's wife: 'Take away from thee the desire of thine eyes,' Blake has introduced one of those recumbent marmoreal figures reminiscent of the royal tombs; another mourning figure, bowed, with falling hair, shows a characteristic pose of Blake's invention.

68

68 *The Death of the Wife of the Biblical Prophet Ezekiel, c.* 1785.

69-77   In 1795 Blake made a series of designs in a new technique, the result of experiments found in certain copies of *Urizen*, probably executed in the previous year. The poet and scholar Lawrence Binyon (1869–1943) described the method Blake used as being 'to make the design roughly and swiftly on mill-board in distemper (not oil-colours) and while it was wet to take an impression from it on paper. The blotted ground-work of this impression was coloured up by hand. The design could be revived on the mill-board when another impression was wanted.' According to Anthony Blunt the medium was probably egg tempera, and the printing was done in two stages, first in a black outline, then in colour. The effect is darker and richer than that of the illuminated books; the texture is mottled.

69   The first of this series is *Elohim [God] creating Adam.* The creator of Adam, the 'mortal worm' or natural man, is Blake's demiurge Urizen; 'thinking as I do that the Creator of this World is a very Cruel Being, and being a Worshipper of Christ, I cannot help saying: "The Son, O how unlike the Father! First God Almighty comes with a Thump on the Head, and then

74   Jesus Christ comes with balm to heal it."' Others in this series

69 OPPOSITE ABOVE *Elohim creating Adam*, 1795–c. 1805.
70 OPPOSITE BELOW *Newton*, 1795–c. 1805.
71 TOP *Nebuchadnezzar*, 1795.
72 ABOVE *The Night of Enitharmon's Joy*, c. 1795.

'Lovely Lambeth'

73 OPPOSITE ABOVE *The House of Death,* 1795–c. 1805.
74 OPPOSITE BELOW *Satan exulting over Eve,* c. 1795.
75 TOP *Pity,* c. 1795.
76 ABOVE *God Judging Adam,* c. 1795, formerly known as *Elijah in the Chariot of Fire.*

70, 71,   are *Satan exulting over Eve*, *Newton*, *Nebuchadnezzar*, *The House*
73, 75   *of Death*, *Hecate*, *Pity, from Macbeth*, *Lamech and his two Wives*,
          The Death of Abel and *Ruth*. The print long known as *Elijah in*
76   *the Chariot of Fire* is now thought to be the supposedly lost
          print of *God judging Adam*.

77   *The Good and Evil Angels*, the last of the series, is, like
          Nebuchadnezzar, developed from a design which first appeared
78   in *The Marriage of Heaven and Hell*. The figures may illustrate
          an idea taken from Blake's admired spiritual master Jakob
          Boehme, who describes the impassable barrier that divides the
          principles of Heaven and Hell as a 'blindness' which prevents
          the devils from seeing the things of Heaven, or the angels those
          of Hell. Even though their worlds should occupy the same place,
          they are in states of being which cannot meet. 'Each Spirit
          is cloathed with his own World's Property wherein it dwells.
          The Beginning of each World's Source is that Limit divides
          one World from the View and Observation of the other.'
70   *Newton* shows the 'spiritual state' of the great scientist; he
          is absorbed in mathematical calculations, his eyes fixed on
          the diagrams he draws on the bottom of that 'sea of time and
          space' which is the principle to which he is confined. Urizen

77 *The Good and Evil Angels*, 1795–c. 1805.

had been similarly represented in one of the plates of *The First Book of Urizen*, immersed in the dark and dense medium of water, traditional esoteric symbol of the material world. Blake invariably uses water and sea in this sense: as Noah's 'flood of the five senses' whose deluge overwhelmed the antediluvian world, from which only the six persons in the Ark survived in the possession of those spiritual faculties which in the Golden Age belonged to all mankind. (For this seemingly roundabout reason, Noah and his Sons, in Blake's mythology, preside over the arts; 'poetry, painting and music' are man's 'three ways of conversing with Paradise'.)

This series of magnificent colour prints marks Blake's full emergence as a master in the visual arts, and as if to mark this independence he also made a series of prints using the metal plates of some of the Lambeth Books without the text, applying colouring to the metal plates to obtain the same mottled effect as that produced by the mill-board.

In a letter written many years later, in 1818, Blake is probably referring to these designs when he speaks of 'a selection from the different Books of such as could be Printed without the Writing, tho' to the Loss of some of the best things. For they when Printed perfect accompany Poetical Personifications & Acts, without which Poems they never could have been Executed.'

Blake's *Small Book of Designs* (1796) was probably made for the miniature-painter Ozias Humphry (1742–1810). His *Large Book of Designs* (*c.* 1796) contains coloured prints of the early works *Joseph of Arimathea* and *Glad Day* (*c.* 1794), the second enlarged 79, 82 from an engraving made in 1780 – the first work to show those inimitable Blakean qualities of joyous energy and elegance of form. Mona Wilson in her *Life* of Blake (1927) suggested that this figure, with its fine wrists and aureole of flaming hair, is a self-portrait. Anthony Blunt saw the pose as suggested by the proportion diagrams of Vincenzo Scamozzi (1548–1616), 81 which Blake would have used as a student. There are similar figures, illustrating the human proportions in relation to square and circle, in Cornelius Agrippa's *Occult Philosophy* 80 (1651), a book Blake had certainly read. The Renaissance conception of the relation of microcosm to macrocosm would have interested so homocentric a thinker as Blake, and reappears in his own depictions and descriptions of 'the Giant Albion', the 'eternal man'.

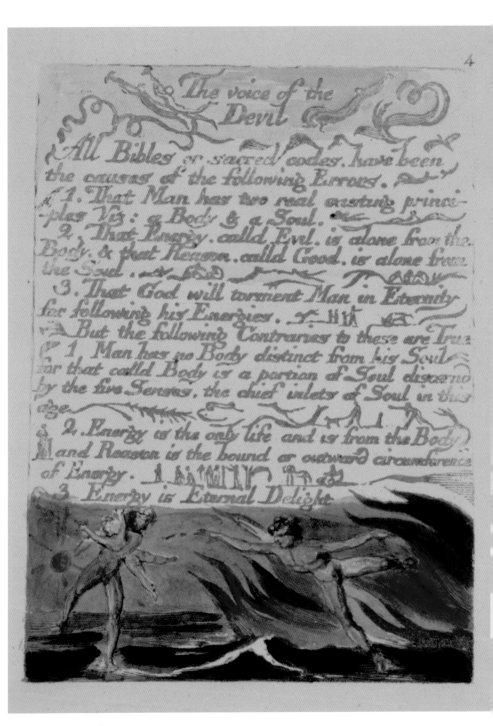

The voice of the
Devil

All Bibles or sacred codes. have been
the causes of the following Errors.
1. That Man has two real existing princi-
-ples Viz: a Body & a Soul.
2. That Energy. calld Evil. is alone from the
Body. & that Reason. calld Good. is alone from
the Soul.
3. That God will torment Man in Eternity
for following his Energies.

But the following Contraries to these are True
1 Man has no Body distinct from his Soul
for that calld Body is a portion of Soul discern'd
by the five Senses. the chief inlets of Soul in this
age.
2. Energy is the only life and is from the Body
and Reason is the bound or outward circumference
of Energy.
3 Energy is Eternal Delight

78 Design for *The Marriage of Heaven and Hell*, c. 1794.
79 *Joseph of Arimathea Preaching to the Britons*, c. 1794–6. Blake's interest in English history extended into legendary prehistory. Joseph of Arimathea is said to have brought Christianity to England, accompanied, some say, by Jesus himself. This legend could give credibility to the lines: 'And did those feet in ancient time/ Walk upon England's mountains green?'

'Lovely Lambeth'

But if the hands be thus elevated , and the feet and Thighes
extended in this manner, by the which a man is made shorter
by the fourteenth part of his upright stature, then the distance
of his feet having reference to the lower belly, they will make
an equilatecall Triangle; and the center being placed in his
navile, a circle being brought about, will touch the ends of
the fingers and toes.

80 Vitruvian man, from Cornelius Agrippa's *Occult Philosophy*, 1651.
81 Drawing, probably after a proportion diagram by Vincenzo Scamozzi,
for *Glad Day*.

82 *Glad Day (The Dance of Albion),*
1794–6.

Chapter 5
Night Thoughts

Blake was by temperament an artist who must follow his own bent. But, always industrious, he accepted whatever work came his way. A commission offered by Edwards, a bookseller, to make and engrave designs to encircle the letter-press of that popular poem of the day, Edward Young's *Night Thoughts* (1742–5), seemed too good to refuse. A contemporary letter gives a glimpse of Blake as a businessman: 'There are about 900 pages. Blake asked 100 guineas for the whole. Edwards said that he could not afford to give more than 20 guineas to which Blake agreed.' For twenty guineas, therefore, Blake made five hundred and thirty-seven designs, of which he engraved fifty-three. These were for the first part of the edition, which was published in the autumn of 1797.

94-6

It may have been Fuseli who proposed Blake to Edwards, for it was he who praised Blake in the book's 'Advertisement', in the highest terms: 'To the eyes of the discerning it need not be pointed out; and while a taste for the arts shall continue to exist, the original conception, and the bold and masterly execution of this artist cannot be unnoticed or unadmired.'

But the project was a disastrous failure, abandoned after the first volume, which did not sell. The original coloured designs are now in the British Museum. In fact, the book is one of Blake's least pleasing works. The heavy designs seem too large and surround an awkward area of type. There is none of the delicacy of Blake's own illuminated books, with insect and tendril lovingly wandering among the lines of verse. His colleagues now began to speak of his 'extravagances', and his 'eccentric designs', with the usual Philistine addition (the words are quoted from the portrait painter John Hoppner, 1758–1810) that: 'Nothing would be more easy than to produce such. They were like the conceits of a drunken fellow or a

83, 84 Pages from the
Vala manuscript, 1797.

85, 86, 87 Pages from *The Four Zoas*, or *Vala*, 1797.

madman.' At least Blake put the proof-pages of Young to good use for the manuscript of his own 'Dream of Nine Nights': *Vala,*

83, 84 or *The Four Zoas.*

It was Blake's fate to be employed as the illustrator of poems far inferior to his own: Robert Blair's *The Grave,* and William Hayley's *Little Tom the Sailor.* Young's poem is the least bad of these best-sellers, whose readers have long gone to those graves which it was their melancholy pleasure to contemplate. For Blake, as for the Neoplatonists, the only grave of the universe was this world, the only death the spiritual death of its benighted inhabitants. He was the last artist to capture the *frisson* and the melancholy of the 'gothic' taste for mortality. And what, one wonders, would the author of *Night Thoughts* have made of Blake's 'Dream of Nine Nights'?

88-93 Another set of illustrations belonging to the Lambeth period, that to Gray's poems, was a labour of love and an example of Blake's 'fun'. It was natural that Blake should have liked Gray; he did so for the same reasons that Dr Johnson, pundit of Augustan taste, disliked him. For in Gray there is the first sound of a new voice, of that 'inspiration' which was to bring to an end the smooth and complacent school of versifiers who preceded the Romantic movement.

It was Gray who in his 'Progress of Poesy' had invoked Shakespeare as supreme creator of:

Such forms as glitter in the Muse's ray
With orient hues, unborrow'd of the Sun...

The style is within the Augustan convention of polished elegance, but the content is new. 'One thing alone makes a poet,' Blake wrote, 'Inspiration, the divine vision.' Gray's interest in the antiquities of England, Wales and Ireland was in harmony both with Blake's interest in English history, and with his passionate mythological eclecticism. Perhaps, too, Blake was right in feeling that Gray's personifications were more than conventional. However that may be, Blake's

91-93 Thames, guardian of the schoolboys of Eton, or his magnificent illustration to Gray's 'The Bard':

Hark, how each giant-oak, and desert cave
Sigh to the torrent's awful voice beneath...

at least shows what he could do as an illustrator of poetry which touched his imagination. His cat and goldfish, illustrating the

89-90 'Ode on the Death of a Favourite Cat', are gay and full of zest. There are 'little winged flies' and flower-elves, reminiscent

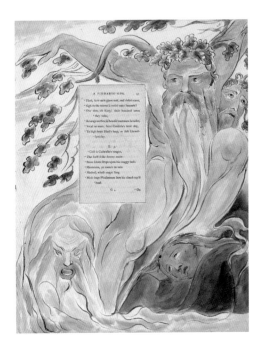

88 Illustration to Gray's
Poems: 'The Bard: A
Pindaric Ode', 1797–8.

of Richard Doyle's (1824–83) later mischievous fancies, and –
somewhat unexpectedly – a perfect observation of the boyish
aristocratic elegance of the Etonians; gained, perhaps, from
the pupils of another school, Westminster, when Blake, a
nameless young draughtsman, was at work among the Abbey
tombs. Blake was obviously moved by the weird mythology of
'The Descent of Odin'; his depictions of the Norns are powerful;
and themes from Gray's Icelandic poem recur in *The Four Zoas*.
The encounter of Urizen and his terrible Daughters in that
poem is evidently based on a passage of Gray which he had
illustrated. But as with all Blake's borrowings, whether from
the Eleusinian Mysteries, Ovid, Swedenborg, or the Bible itself,
the transformation is so radical that the seminal image is
completely transformed.

Blake seems to have had no thought of publishing his
illustrations to Gray's poems; eventually he presented the
volume to Flaxman's wife as a mark of gratitude for yet another
disastrous attempt to 'help' him, which was to lead to his
removal from London during the years 1800–3: Flaxman's
introduction of the poet to Hayley, 'the hermit of Eartham'.

89, 90 OPPOSITE Illustrations to Gray's 'Ode on the Death of a Favourite Cat', 1797–8.

O D E

ON THE DEATH OF A

FAVOURITE CAT.

Drowned in a Tub of Gold Fishes.

'TWAS on a lofty vase's side,
    Where China's gayest art had dy'd
The azure flowers, that blow;
Demurest of the tabby kind,
The pensive Selima reclin'd,
    Gaz'd on the lake below.

Her conscious tail her joy declar'd;
The fair round face, the snowy beard,
    The velvet of her paws,
        D 4   Her

O D E

ON THE DEATH OF A

FAVOURITE CAT.

Drowned in a Tub of Gold Fishes.

D 2

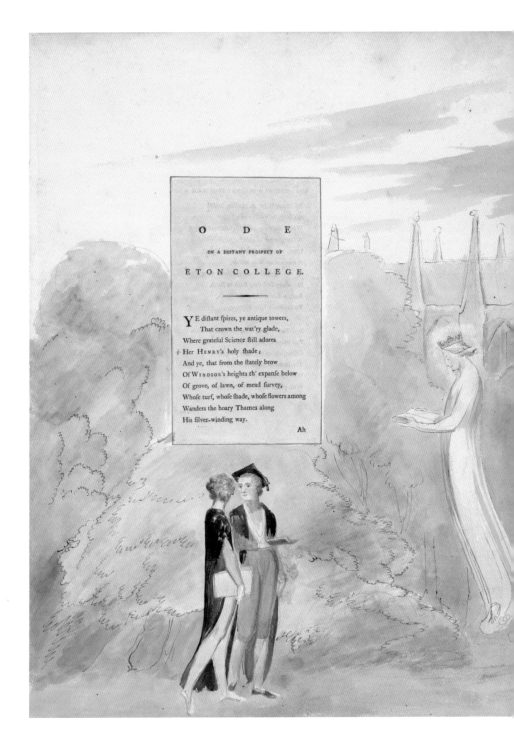

O D E

ON A DISTANT PROSPECT OF

E T O N   C O L L E G E.

Y E diſtant ſpires, ye antique towers,
    That crown the wat'ry glade,
Where grateful Science ſtill adores
+ Her HENRY's holy ſhade;
And ye, that from the ſtately brow
Of WINDSOR's heights th' expanſe below
Of grove, of lawn, of mead ſurvey,
Whoſe turf, whoſe ſhade, whoſe flowers among
Wanders the hoary Thames along
His ſilver-winding way.

Ah

91-3 Illustrations to Gray's 'On a Distant Prospect of Eton College', 1797–8.

94 OPPOSITE Edward Young's *Night Thoughts, c.* 1797. Title-page of 'Night the First'.
95 TOP *Night Thoughts,* c. 1797. 'The Christian Triumph'.
96 RIGHT *Night Thoughts,* c. 1797. 'Where sense runs savage broke from reason's chain'.

Night Thoughts

Chapter 6
Natural Friends

Blake once wrote, in a moment of exasperation, that 'natural friends are spiritual enemies'. He was thinking at the time of Hayley's misguided attempts at patronage. George Cumberland, too, had tried to help Blake, introducing him to a clergyman, a Dr Trusler, who was in search of 'moral paintings' to illustrate a new book. But as Blake wrote to Cumberland in August 1799: 'I have made him a Drawing in my best manner; he has sent it back with a Letter full of Criticisms, in which he says It accords not with his Intentions, which are to Reject all Fancy from his Work. How far he Expects to please I cannot tell. But as I cannot paint Dirty rags & old shoes when I ought to place Naked Beauty or simple ornament, I despair of Ever pleasing one class of Men. Unfortunately our authors of books are among this Class; how soon we shall have a change for the better I cannot Prophecy. Dr Trusler says "*Your Fancy*, from what I have seen of it, & I have seen variety at Mr Cumberland's, seems to be in the other world, or the World of Spirits, which accords not with my Intentions, which, whilst living in This World, Wish to follow *the Nature of it.*" I could not help smiling at the difference between the doctrines of Dr Trusler & those of Christ.'

But we owe to the Reverend Doctor some thanks for having elicited from Blake, if not one of his best designs, certainly one of his finest letters. Blake begins, 'I really am sorry that you are fall'n out with the Spiritual World'; and continues:

'I have therefore proved your Reasonings Ill proportion'd, which you can never prove my figures to be; they are those of Michael Angelo, Rafael & the Antique, & of the best living Models. I percieve [sic] that your Eye is perverted by Caricature Prints, which ought not to abound as much as they do. Fun I love, but too much Fun is of all things most loathsom. Mirth is better than Fun, & Happiness is better than Mirth. I feel that a Man may be happy in This World. And I know that This World Is a World of Imagination & Vision. I see Everything I paint In This World, but Everybody does not see alike. To the Eyes of a Miser a Guinea is far more beautiful than the Sun, & a bag worn with the use of Money has more beautiful proportions than a Vine filled with Grapes. The tree which moves some to tears of joy is in the Eyes of others only a Green thing which stands in the way. Some see Nature all Ridicule & Deformity, & by these I shall not regulate my proportions; & some scarce see Nature at all. But to the Eyes of the Man of Imagination, Nature is Imagination itself. As a man is, So he sees. As the Eye is formed, such are its Powers. You certainly Mistake, when you say that the Visions of Fancy are not to be found in This World. To Me This World is all One continued Vision of Fancy or Imagination, & I feel Flatter'd when I am told so. What is it that sets Homer, Virgil & Milton in so high a rank of Art? Why is the Bible more Entertaining & Instructive than any other book? Is it not because they are addressed to the Imagination, which is Spiritual Sensation, & but mediately to the Understanding or Reason? Such is True Painting, and such was alone valued by the Greeks & the best modern Artists.' On this letter Trusler wrote: 'Blake, dim'd with Superstition.'

One can imagine how Blake must have shrunk from the caricaturist Thomas Rowlandson's (1756–1827) gross hideosities, to which he refers in his letter to Cumberland: 'for his own sake I am sorry to see that a Man [Dr Trusler] should be so enamour'd of Rowlandson's caricatures as to call them copies of life & manners'. As so often happens, a society which will accept the distortions of degradation, calls mad, extravagant, fanciful and so on, the rectifications of nature whose intention is in accordance with some norm of beauty – the elongations of Gothic statuary, or these departures from the proportions of 'the naked' by which the Renaissance sculptors (as Sir Kenneth Clark showed in a study of 1956) arrived at the fitting proportions of 'the nude'. The way down is, on every level, easier than the way up; and the public of eighteenth-century England was, when all is said, coarse and provincial.

But Blake had one patron who never failed him, who left him free to follow his own imaginative impulse, promising only to buy from him whatever he should paint. This was Thomas Butts (1757–1845), who is first referred to by Blake in the letter to George Cumberland already quoted:

'As to Myself, about whom you are so kindly Interested, I live by Miracle. I am Painting small Pictures from the Bible. For as to Engraving, in which art I cannot reproach myself with any neglect, yet I am laid in a corner as if I did not Exist, & Since my Young's Night Thoughts have been publish'd, Even Johnson & Fuseli have discarded my Graver. But as I know that He who Works & has his health cannot starve, I laugh at Fortune & Go on & on. I think I forsee better Things than I have ever seen. My Work pleases my employer, and I have an order for Fifty small Pictures at One Guinea each, which is Something better than mere copying after another artist.'

Blake's 'employer' filled his house in Fitzroy Square with his works: Butts' house was to be the chief repository of Blake's output as a painter to the end of his life. Geoffrey Keynes described him as 'a dumb admirer of genius, which he could see but not quite understand'. The greater his honour, if this be so, for his lifelong and single-minded devotion, honouring, as Blake says we should, the gifts of the spirit in other men. Gilchrist said he was 'Muster-master General'; but the Blake scholar G. E. Bentley, Jr (1930–2017) found that he was in fact only chief clerk in the Muster-master's office, writing the letters dealing with the enlistment of soldiers. He did, however, die a wealthy man, probably having made his fortune by wise investment and in real estate.

Butts was more than a purchaser; to him Blake could open his heart, as we know from many letters addressed to him. Mr and Mrs Blake were frequent and welcome guests at the house in Fitzroy Square; and Butts even tactfully sought to increase Blake's income by sending his son Thomas to take drawing lessons. 'Tommy' must have been a secret rebel; on inheriting his father's Blake collection he sold a great part of it, including the original *Illustrations of the Book of Job.* The remainder he left to his son, Captain Butts, and his daughter, Mrs Graham Foster Piggot. Mrs Piggot stored her share in a loft where they are said to have been 'devoured by rats'; but Captain Butts appreciated Blake's work, and his share of the great Blake collection remained almost intact. His widow was obliged to sell the collection in 1903, by which time Blake's fame was beginning to rise. These pictures were bought by the painter Graham Robertson (1866–1948), who between 1885 and 1940 was Blake's most devoted and discerning collector. At the sale of his collection in 1949, many of Blake's greatest works went to public galleries. Graham Robertson had himself bequeathed seven, including five of the colour-printed drawings, to the Tate Gallery; and he left a fund to enable paintings to be bought for public collections.

97 *The Body of Christ Borne to the Tomb, c.* 1799–1800, one of Blake's many works for Thomas Butts.
98 *Job and his Daughters,* 1799–1800.

99 OPPOSITE ABOVE *The Angel Appearing to Zacharias*, 1799–1800.
100 OPPOSITE BELOW *Christ Giving Sight to Bartimaeus*, 1799–1800.
101 ABOVE *Mary Magdalene Washing Christ's Feet*, c. 1805.

Natural Friends

102 *Mary Magdalene at the Sepulchre, c.* 1805.
103 *Jephthah Met by his Daughter, c.* 1803.

Natural Friends

Nearly all Blake's surviving Bible illustrations, in tempera, watercolour and colour-printed drawing, come from the Butts collection. They number one hundred and thirty-seven illustrations of Old Testament subjects and thirty-eight of the New Testament. Blake was selling regularly to Butts between 1799 and 1810. He writes to him with justifiable pride: 'the works I have done for You are Equal to Carrache or Rafael (and I am now Seven years older than Rafael was when he died), I say they are Equal to Carrache or Rafael, or Else I am Blind, Stupid, Ignorant and Incapable in two years' Study to understand those things which a Boarding School Miss can comprehend in a fortnight. Be assured, My dear Friend, that there is not one touch in these Drawings & Pictures but what came from my Head & my Heart in Unison; That I am Proud of being their Author and Grateful to you my Employer; & that I look upon you as the Chief of my Friends, whom I would endeavour to please, because you, among all men, have enabled me to produce these things.'

Blake had an antipathy to the oil medium because he thought it would not stand the test of time; 'oil became a fetter to genius, and a dungeon to art', he declared. He used what he called 'tempera', because he believed 'the colours would be as pure and permanent as precious stones', like those early Italian paintings he most admired. Unfortunately he was wrong. His temperas, painted on canvas, wood and sometimes on copper, were applied, not in egg medium, such as the Italian masters used, but in a solution of glue, with a light wash of glue laid on afterwards as varnish. All have darkened and cracked, and many have not survived. He must have improved his tempera technique, however, for the later paintings in this medium (for example the Arlington Court tempera, and *Ugolino and his sons in Prison*) have not suffered to the same extent. Not until 1941 was a method of cleaning and laying down the surfaces discovered, making possible their restoration and preservation.

Few of Blake's paintings are more than two feet square: they are 'small pictures' to hang on the walls of his patron's house. England neglected the talent of her greatest religious artist, who would have rejoiced to decorate the churches of London, making their walls brilliant as the Gothic mural painters had done. George Goyder, in his Introduction to the William Blake Trust illustrated catalogue of Blake's Bible illustrations (1957), writes that: 'It was Blake's ambition to make England, like Italy, "respected on account of art"'. Some years ago Heming Vaughan tried to set in train a project of a Blake Bible; perhaps the project may be revived someday, for no other English artist has illustrated the Bible with comparable understanding.

104 *The Soldiers casting Lots for Christ's Garments*, 1800.

Natural Friends

It was through no wish of his own that Blake worked in seclusion. In his *Descriptive Catalogue* of 1809 he lamented that the painters of England were not engaged on public works. Four of the Bible series, his magnificent *Jacob's Ladder*, *The Body of Abel found by Adam and Eve*, *Soldiers casting Lots for Christ's Garments* and *Angels Hovering* were designed as frescoes to adorn the altars of churches. These frescoes were to be removable, for 'If the Frescos of *Apelles*, of *Protogenes*, of *Raphael* or *Michael Angelo* could have been removed, we might, perhaps, have them now in England. I could divide Westminster Hall, or the walls of any other great Building, into compartments and ornament them with Frescos, which would be removable at pleasure.'

119
112,
104

So wrote Blake on 'The Invention of a Portable Fresco' in the advertisement for his one public exhibition, his last vain attempt to persuade the visionless patrons of contemporary English art to allow him to adorn our public buildings and churches.

Chapter 7
The Line of
the Almighty

In a lecture given at the Italian Institute in London in 1958, Italian literary critic Giorgio Melchiori (1920–2009) answered many of the questions which arise from Blake's professions of enthusiastic admiration for Michelangelo. What did Blake learn from Michelangelo? Did he understand, or profoundly misunderstand, the master whose work he had never seen in the original, but only in engravings? Since Blake had never seen Michelangelo's sculpture, it is understandable that he should have seen his work in linear terms. But he was, in any case, a linear artist in practice and by conviction. The painter Roger Fry (1866–1934), who did not like the linear, or Blake, nevertheless (according to Professor Melchiori) 'put the question of Blake's style in a nutshell: "Blake translated Michelangelo into mere line, line which does not evoke volume at all, but remains pure line; and he lets his lines wave about in those meandering, nerveless curves which were so beloved by Celtic craftsmen long before."'

'Nerveless curves' is equally insensitive as a description of Blake's line and of Celtic craftsmanship. Line was, for Blake, above all an expression of energy. Every solid form can be seen as the imprint and the product of a flow of energy, and it is certain that Blake saw line as energy, as the signature of life.

'The great and golden rule of art, as well as of life, is this,' he wrote: 'That the more distinct, sharp, and wiry the bounding line, the more perfect the work of art; and the less keen and sharp, the greater is the evidence of weak imitation, plagiarism, and bungling. Great inventors, in all ages, knew this: Protogenes and Apelles knew each other by this line. Rafael and Michael Angelo and Albert Dürer are known by this and this alone. The want of this determinate and bounding form evidences the want of idea in the artist's mind, and the pretence of the plagiary in all its branches. How do we distinguish the oak from the beech, the horse from the ox, but by the bounding outline? How do we distinguish one face or countenance from another, but by the bounding line and its infinite inflexions and movements? What is it that builds a house and plants a garden, but the definite and determinate? What is it that distinguishes honesty from knavery, but the hard and wirey line of rectitude and certainty in the actions and intentions? Leave out this line, and you leave out life itself; all is chaos again, and the line of the almighty must be drawn out upon it before man or beast can exist.'

Hogarth had discovered the 'line of beauty' in the waving or serpentine line, the meander, and as Professor Melchiori relates, 'he was delighted when a friend pointed out to him that his theory of the pre-eminence of the serpentine line corresponded exactly to a precept of Michelangelo's'. In his preface to his *Analysis of Beauty* (1753), Hogarth quoted from G. P. Lomazzo's treatise on painting (in an English translation of 1598) the passage in which Michelangelo's view is given. Blake must have read Hogarth's work, and, finding in Michelangelo what he had discerned in Gothic, and Flaxman in Greek art, he added Michelangelo to the circle of those spiritual friends (like Boehme and Paracelsus, Socrates, Milton and the Hebrew prophets) who sometimes 'dined with him' on 'the bread of sweet thought and the wine of delight'. According to Lomazzo: 'It is reported that Michael Angelo upon a time gave this observation to the Painter *Marcus da Sciena*, his scholler: that he should alwaies make a figure Pyramidall, Serpent like, and multiplied by one two and three. In which precept (in mine opinion) the whole mysterie of the arte consisteth. For the greatest grace and life that a picture can have, is, that it expresses Motion: which the Painters call the Spirite of a picture. Nowe there is no forme so fitte to expresse this *motion*, as that of the flame of the fire, which according to *Aristotle* and the other Philosophers, is an elemente most active of all others; because the forme of the flame thereof is most apt for motion: for it hath a *Conus* or sharpe pointe wherewith it seemeth to divide the aire, that so it may ascend to his proper sphere. So that a picture having this forme will be most beautiful.'

If for no other reason, Blake would have loved Michelangelo for the observation in this passage. For Blake, volume and weight belonged to the mechanistic concept of a natural world subject to the quantitative 'laws of nature' as these operate in time and space; the universe of 'Bacon, Newton and Locke', of the 'Satanic mills' of natural causality – to all, in fact, which he himself opposed with all the energy of his prophetic mission. Against the mechanistic view of nature, product of the rational mind of Urizen, Blake proclaimed life. Life is non-spatial and non-temporal; gravity does not weigh it down, nor bulk contain it. There are, for Blake's human figures, essentially two conditions – the unconfined freedom of unimpeded energy; and the constricted, fettered, weighted and cramped state of the prisoners of Urizen's universe of mechanized nature. Michelangelo's prisoners, struggling from their rocky confinement, would have signified, for Blake, life freeing itself from the oppression of matter, like the figure of Earth in his own *Gates of Paradise.*

Even had Blake seen Michelangelo in the original, it is not possible to imagine that he would have followed him in mass and volume, since these had no part in his own imaginative vision. The figures of a spiritual art, whether Gothic, Byzantine or Buddhist, whether of men or angels, are situated in mental, not corporeal, space. The weightlessness of a Chinese landscape likewise expresses a vision of nature unconditioned by physical bulk and volume. The naturalism of Western European art, against whose restrictions Blake was in revolt, is indeed rather the exception than the rule in the art of the world.

The spirit is already free; and 'the spiritual body or angel' is the true man, released from its 'excrementitious husk and covering'. Here Blake is close to Swedenborg, whose disembodied spirits are fully human but liberated from the restrictions of a material body. Swedenborg taught that the Resurrection of the Dead is the freeing of the spiritual body from its earthly envelope, the 'rotten rags' of mortality. Like Swedenborg, Blake had himself seen spirits of another plane of existence: his brother Robert, 'clapping his hands for joy' as he rose through the ceiling, and other spiritual visitants, real or imagined, throughout his life. The physical body was beautiful to Blake in so far as it reflected the lineaments of an informing soul or spirit, the 'celestial body' of a famous passage of St Paul's First Epistle to the Corinthians, which Blake invokes in his emblem accompanying the poem 'To Tirzah' (*c.* 1801): *It is raised a spiritual body.* Blake's human figures are already such. 'Man has no Body distinct from his Soul; for that call'd Body is a portion of Soul discern'd by the five senses.' He held that 'the Poetic Genius is the true Man, and that the body or outward form of Man is derived from the Poetic Genius'.

Like Plato, Blake uses the symbol of the Cave. For him the Cave is the body, lit by the five windows of the senses. 'If the doors of perception were cleansed every thing would appear to man as it is, infinite. For man has closed himself up, till he sees all things thro' narrow chinks of his cavern.'

105

This traditional esoteric teaching seemed strange to Blake's contemporaries, and seems scarcely less so to ours.

Blake by no means shared the British love of landscape painting. He loved natural forms – tendril and leaf, and the stranger forms of insect, worm and spider – as he did the human, but these he loved as embodiments of life. 'Everything that lives is holy', from 'the little winged fly' to man. The generalized impression of landscape was by no means the way in which Blake saw nature. For him the 'minute particulars' were all-important, and form the boundaries of some living energy. For Blake, all is human, since in this world man is central, made in the 'image of God', as the microcosm:

Each grain of Sand,
Every Stone on the Land,
Each rock & each hill,
Each fountain & rill,
Each herb & each tree,
Mountain, hill, earth & sea,
Cloud, Meteor & Star,
Are Men Seen Afar.

Blake returns to a concept fundamental in all spiritual traditions: man is not 'part of nature', but all natural phenomena have their existence in consciousness. The human world is the world presented by human consciousness. He invokes the symbolic Adam Kadmon, of the Jewish esoteric tradition:

'You [the Jews] have a tradition that Man anciently contain'd in his mighty limbs all things in Heaven & Earth: this you received from the Druids.

'But now the Starry Heavens are fled from the mighty limbs of Albion.'

The universe of Newtonian science Blake condemned as a universe of abstractions and formulae, not of experience. Man's earth is what he perceives; and, as such, 'though it appears without, it is within/In your Imagination'. In a Michelangelesque figure Blake illustrates Albion's 'mighty limbs' with sun, moon and stars, about to be externalized by the 'cruel' female principle of nature:

Thou Mother of my Mortal part
With cruelty didst mould my Heart
And with false self-deceiving tears
Didst bind my Nostrils, Eyes and Ears:
Didst close my Tongue in senseless clay,
And me to Mortal Life betray.

106

105 *Songs of Experience*, c. 1825. 'To Tirzah.'

Since the City is the expression of humanity, Blake's (or the Giant Albion's) 'Great Work' is the building of the 'spiritual fourfold London':

... for Cities
Are Men, fathers of multitudes, & Rivers & Mountains
Are also Men; everything is Human, mighty! sublime!

That which Blake and the Florentine painters, Raphael and Michelangelo in particular, have in common is in reality the Neoplatonic – and specifically Plotinian – aesthetics, upon which the concept of 'ideal form' depends; identified by Blake, of course, with his 'divine humanity': 'To whom all lineaments tend and seek in love & sympathy.'

Whether from his early training, or from the fact of being a Londoner, or for deeper reasons, 'the human form divine' was for Blake at all times supreme.

Political theorist Edmund Burke (1729–97) in *A Philosophical Enquiry into the Origin of the Sublime and the Beautiful* (1757) had drawn a distinction which gave rise to a style common to Blake and his contemporaries, intended to express 'the sublime' as distinct from 'the beautiful'. According to Burke, the basis of beauty is pleasure; that of sublimity, pain. Obscurity, grandeur, disorder, terror, power, vastness, infinity, difficulty and magnificence, by producing painful impressions, lead to

106 *Jerusalem*, 1804–20, Plate 25. Note sun, moon and stars on the body of the Cosmic Man.

the sublime. Blake rejected Burke's application of these ideas to picturesque landscape; but in common with Barry, Fuseli, Stothard and other contemporaries, he was not slow to attempt 'the sublime' in terms of the human form. Anthony Blunt points out that Blake, Barry, Stothard and Fuseli all attempted an example cited by Burke in illustration of his meaning,

107   Milton's description in *Paradise Lost* of Satan, Sin and Death. In this context the grandeur and *terribilità* of Michelangelo takes its natural place. Those tormented and falling figures of his *Last Judgment* were the source of many visual themes to be found in Blake, including his own *Last Judgment*. Professor Melchiori suggested that Blake's 'visions' of the Four Zoas are re-creations, probably unconscious, of the Michelangelesque works with which he was familiar. Blake's visual memory for both words and pictorial themes was remarkable, as anyone who studies his works soon discovers. Anthony Blunt has described many such visual borrowings; and the present author was guided in the discovery of many of Blake's literary sources by the 'minute particulars' of word and phrase borrowed – again probably unconsciously – from works he loved.

Blake's Bible illustrations, many of which were made during his residence at Lambeth, are unequal in quality. Anthony Blunt thinks that Blake's early choice of Biblical theme sometimes tended to underline his revolutionary views on sexual morality: there were, for instance, his *David and Bathsheba, Potiphar's Wife, Susannah and the Elders.* Be this as it may, each will find among them what he seeks. To the present writer, those

69   profoundly esoteric depictions of the Seven Spirits of God –
108   *The Creation of Light, God creating Adam, The Lord answers*
109   *Job out of the Whirlwind, David delivered out of Many Waters*
110   or *Ezekiel's Vision* – speak of spiritual mysteries in a pictorial language lost since the Ages of Faith. There is the superb heavenly ladder of Jacob's dream with its ascending and descending angels; the paradisal beauty of *Adam naming the Beasts* and *Eve naming the Birds.* The fleeing figure of Cain in

112   *The Body of Abel found by Adam and Eve* is almost Expressionist
111   in quality, and the desolate dream-landscape of *Famine* anticipates the best of Surrealism. Fine as are many of Blake's more naturalistic paintings, these might have been the work of one or other of his contemporaries; those of the interior vision, no one but Blake could then have attempted.

Of his New Testament subjects, few are more beautiful
113   than his depictions of the Holy Child. In *The Nativity*, a child enveloped in light (as Orc in his flames) hovers above the reclining figure of the Virgin, conveying, as in no other painting known to me, the realization that the Christ-child

who 'descends' into generation comes not from the Virgin's womb but from another order of being. Similarly with the Adoration of the Kings and Christ asleep on the Cross. For Blake the Holy Child is not so much one of those Renaissance descendants of the Classical Eros so beloved by the Italian schools, as the *multum in parvo* of a spiritual mystery:

And Jehovah stood in the Gates of the Victim, & he appeared
A weeping Infant in the Gates of Birth in the midst of Heaven.

Both Virgin and Child of Blake's 'black' Madonna seem closer in spirit to Early Christian art than to any post-Renaissance work.

Blake's depictions of Jesus as a man, on the other hand, have all too much in common with those sentimental Counter-Reformation illustrations associated with the cult of the Sacred Heart. But there are magnificent exceptions: above all, the majestic tragedy of *The Agony in the Garden*, with the grandeur of the descending angel who supports the figure of Christ. The *Last Supper* invites, and sustains, comparison with those Italian masters Blake admired. The lyrical *Wise and Foolish Virgins* is

114

122

115

107 OPPOSITE Illustration to *Paradise Lost,* 1807. 'Satan, Sin and Death.'
108 ABOVE *The Lord answers Job out of the Whirlwind,* c. 1799.

The Line of the Almighty

109 *David delivered out of Many Waters*, c. 1805.
110 *The Whirlwind: Ezekiel's Vision of the Cherubim and Eyed Wheels*, c. 1803–5.

The Line of the Almighty

one of the most beautiful illustrations of parable. Again, with
116
his illustrations to the *Book of Revelation* (*The Angel Michael
117
Binding Satan* or *The River of Life*), Blake is in his true element
of 'spiritual vision'.

118
    The Last Judgment – on the last of several versions of
which Blake continued to work until the time of his death –
has a character altogether unprecedented. Both this work
and the closely related *Meditation among the Tombs* have a
diagrammatic structure more common in Tibetan Buddhist art
than in Christian iconography. The flowing figures, ascending
to the radiant Christ Enthroned, or falling headlong into Hell
as in Michelangelo's *Last Judgment*, seem less like individuals
than cells circulating in the life-stream of cosmic life. While
for single figures or groups of figures we can find parallels in
works by Michelangelo, for the composition as a whole I know
none later than the Gothic Middle Ages. We are reminded by
this work that Blake was a Swedenborgian; his *Judgment* is
a superb depiction of Swedenborg's conception of the Grand
Man, prototype of Blake's own 'divine humanity' or 'Jesus,
the Imagination', the one God in all, and the all in the One.

    From an aesthetic point of view, it was unfortunate for Blake
that the tradition within which he was working offered him
no precedent. We see the grandeur of his conception through
the medium of an almost primitive clumsiness. Comparison
with those Tibetan painted mandalas, which (though Blake
never saw them) are depictions of similar spiritual realization,
demonstrates the immense advantage of an inherited
traditional language. Blake's spiritual vision – Swedenborg's
also, it may be – needed – demanded – a new form; but it
was too much for a solitary artist to create, against the trend
161-8
of history, a new pictorial language. In his *Job* engravings,
indeed, Blake went far towards creating such a language –
one in which he has had no successors. It may be that the
New Age of which he knew himself a prophet will yet discover
in Blake the forerunner of a new way of expressing the non-
spatial interpenetration of spiritual worlds, and that spiritual
collectivity of life of which he had so strong an intuition.

    Perhaps it is because Blake's Jesus is so essentially the one
God in all, rather than the Jesus of history, that his imagination
takes fire in his great Judgment more than in his illustrations
of episodes in the life of Christ. His two magnificent
descriptions of the composition give us in some ways a clearer

111 *Famine*, 1805.
112 *The Body of Abel found by Adam and Eve*, c. 1826. Cain, who was about to bury
the body, flees from the face of his parents.

113 TOP *The Nativity, c.* 1799–1800.
114 ABOVE *The Agony in the Garden, c.* 1799–1800.
115 OPPOSITE ABOVE *The Parable of the Wise and Foolish Virgins, c.* 1799–1800.
116 OPPOSITE BELOW *The Angel Michael Binding Satan, c.* 1805.

117 *The River of Life, c.* 1805.
118 *Last Judgment* (the watercolour version in the Petworth Collection), 1808.

The Line of the Almighty

view of the grandeur of his vision than do the two surviving versions, or the drawings:

'The Last Judgment is not Fable or Allegory, but Vision.... The Hebrew Bible & the Gospel of Jesus are not Allegory, but Eternal Vision or Imagination of All that Exists.... The Last Judgment is one of these Stupendous Visions. I have represented it as I saw it; to different People it appears differently as everything else does; for tho' on Earth things seem Permanent, they are less permanent than a Shadow, as we all know too well....

'This world of Imagination is the world of Eternity; it is the divine bosom into which we shall all go after the death of the Vegetated body. This World of Imagination is Infinite & Eternal, whereas the world of Generation, or Vegetation, is Finite & Temporal. There Exist in that Eternal World the Permanent Realities of Every Thing which we see reflected in this Vegetable Glass of Nature. All Things are comprehended in their Eternal Forms in the divine body of the Saviour, the True Vine of Eternity, the Human Imagination, who appear'd to Me as Coming to Judgment among his Saints & throwing off the Temporal that the Eternal might be Establish'd; round him were seen the Images of Existences according to a certain order Suited to my Imaginative Eye....'

There follows a detailed account of the various groups of figures.

This conception of the collective Being of the 'divine humanity' is already clearly stated in *The Four Zoas*:

Then those in Great Eternity met in the Council of God
As one Man, for contracting their Exalted Senses
They behold Multitude, or Expanding they behold as one,
As One Man all the Universal family; & that One Man
They call Jesus the Christ, & they in him & he in them
Live in perfect harmony, in Eden the land of life,
Consulting as One Man above the Mountain of Snowdon
    Sublime.

It may well be a stumbling block to art critics that Blake so greatly admired the diagrams in William Law's edition of Jakob Boehme (1764), where, as W. B. Yeats (himself the author of a comparably bewildering mystical structure) wrote, 'one lifts a flap of paper to discover both the human entrails and starry heavens. William Blake thought these diagrams worthy of Michael Angelo, but remains himself almost unintelligible because he never drew the like.' *The Last Judgment* is the nearest Blake came to a visual depiction of his spiritual cosmos; but

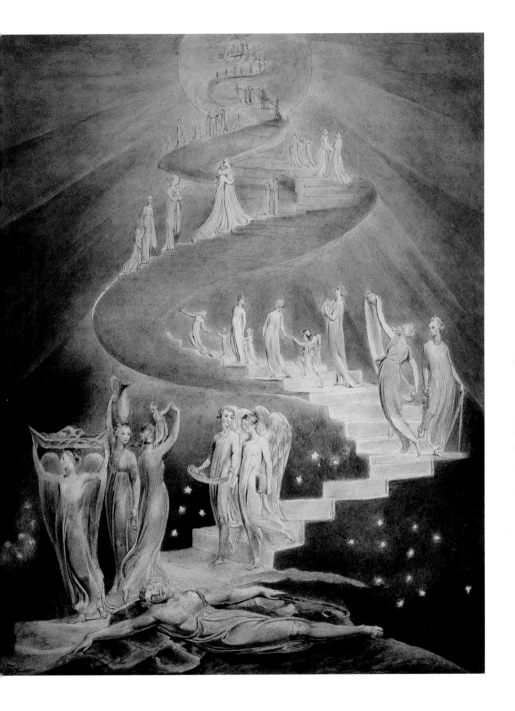

119 *Jacob's Ladder, c.* 1799–1806.

The Line of the Almighty

120 *Angel of the Divine Presence Bringing Eve to Adam, c.* 1803.
121 *The Archangel Raphael with Adam and Eve,* from *Paradise Lost,* 1808.

The Line of the Almighty   **143**

122 *The Last Supper*, 1799.

long passages in both *The Four Zoas* and *Jerusalem* describe the 'fourfold' interior city. S. Foster Damon in his *Blake Dictionary* (1965) drew a chart of Golgonooza: a square within a circle from whose central 'Throne of God' creation issues – a diagram of a type familiar to students of Carl Jung, and called (by analogy with Tibetan Buddhist art) a 'mandala'. Jung's patients often produced these 'mandalas' in the course of analysis, as symbols of the integration of the psyche. Far from suggesting that Blake's 'mandalas' are an expression of his personal imbalance, I wish only to draw attention to the diagrammatic character of a certain kind of vision; that, for example, of Ezekiel's Wheels, or the Four Living Creatures round the Throne; of the Apocalyptic City of St John the Divine; or indeed of Dante's Mountain of Hell and Purgatory. To these visionaries Blake himself often turned, as to his imaginative next of kin.

Chapter 8
Spiritual Enemies

William Hayley was a country gentleman whose eccentricity
was the writing and publishing of verse. His poetry was
perhaps no worse than a great deal of bad verse now forgotten;
it is chiefly for his life of his friend William Cowper that he
is remembered in his own right. His natural son, Thomas
Adolphus, was for a time apprenticed to Flaxman as a sculptor.
After his son's death in 1800 he engaged Blake to make an
engraving of the boy's head. Hayley was not particularly pleased
with this work – he was always given to meddling with artists
he had himself commissioned, even 'improving' Flaxman's
designs for him – but he may have been touched by the letter
Blake wrote to him about his son:

'Thirteen years ago I lost a brother & with his spirit I converse
daily & hourly in the Spirit & See him in my remembrance in
the regions of my imagination. I hear his advice & even now
write from his Dictate. Forgive me for Expressing to you my
Enthusiasm which I wish all to partake of Since it is to me
a Source of Immortal Joy: even in this world by it I am the
companion of Angels. May you continue to be so more & more
& to be more & more persuaded that every Mortal loss is an
Immortal Gain. The Ruins of Time builds Mansions
in Eternity.'

Flaxman suggested to Hayley that he should employ Blake
as the engraver of the plates for his proposed life of Cowper;
and that he might, incidentally, be able to assist him to obtain
other work by introductions to his friends. Both Hayley and
Blake welcomed Flaxman's suggestion that Blake should move
to the village of Felpham, in Sussex, near Hayley's residence at
Eartham. Yet, as Mona Wilson observes in her *Life*, Blake might
have accounted his corporeal friend Flaxman a spiritual enemy
had he seen a letter he wrote to Hayley: 'You may naturally

suppose that I am highly pleased with the exertion of your usual Benevolence in favour of my friend Blake, & as such an occasion offers you will perhaps be more satisfied in having the portraits engraved under your own eye, than at a distance, indeed I hope that Blake's residence at Felpham will be a mutual comfort to you & him, & I see no reason why he should not make as good a livelihood there as in London, if he engraves & teaches drawing, by which he may gain considerably, as also by making neat drawings of different kinds, but if he places any dependence on painting large pictures, for which he is not qualified either by habit or study, he will be miserably deceived.'

Had Flaxman written in a different vein, would Hayley perhaps have refrained from the well-meant discouragement which he seems to have given from the first to Blake's grander ideas? Was he, in finding Blake commissions to paint miniatures of his friends, conscientiously carrying out Flaxman's instructions? 'Neat drawings of different kinds' were the last thing for which Blake's genius fitted him, unless we so describe his sublime *Job* series. If Hayley's kindness was misdirected from the outset, was it not in part the fault of Flaxman? Blake, in gratitude, wrote in terms which put Flaxman to shame:

'You, O Dear Flaxman, are a Sublime Archangel, My Friend & Companion from Eternity; in the Divine bosom in our Dwelling place. I look back into the regions of Reminiscence & behold our ancient days before this Earth appear'd in its vegetated mortality to my mortal vegetated Eyes. I see our houses in Eternity, which can never be separated, tho' our Mortal vehicles should stand at the remotest corners of heaven from each other.'

Hayley kept 'our good Blake' busy with this and that, conscientiously trying to fill his time so that he should not indulge in 'visions'. Blake worked on the engraving of the plates for the life of Cowper, besides making a series of medallion heads of the poets for Hayley's library. For a broadsheet, *Little Tom the Sailor* (the poem written by Hayley), Blake made head- and tail-pieces; the broadsheet was to be sold as a charity for the widowed mother of the boy. Hayley's *Ballads*, with illustrations by Blake, were to be sold for Blake's own profit; but the venture was a financial failure. The poet Robert Southey (1774–1843) in a review ridicules Hayley's verses, and adds a word on the illustrator:

'The poet has had the singular good fortune to meet with a painter capable of doing full justice to his conceptions; and,

123 OPPOSITE ABOVE LEFT Illustration for Hayley's *Ballads*. *The Horse*, 1805.
124 OPPOSITE ABOVE RIGHT Illustration for Hayley's *Ballads*. Frontispiece: *The Hermit's Dog*, 1805.
125 OPPOSITE BELOW Illustration for Hayley's *Ballads*. *The Eagle*, 1805.

The Horse

Pub.d June 18 1805 by R. Phillips N.o 6 Bridge Street Black Friers

The Dog

Pub.d June 18. 1805 by R. Phillips N.o 6. Bridge Street Black Friers

The Eagle

Pub.d June 18 1805 by R. Phillips N.o 6 Bridge Street Black Friers in fact, when we look at the delectable frontispiece to this volume, which represents Edward starting back, Fido *volant*, and the crocodile *rampant*, with a mouth open like a bootjack to receive him we know not whether most to admire the genius of Mr William Blake or of Mr William Hayley.'

One can see what Southey means; the picture is very funny but it was not meant to be. If Blake can be blamed, it is for not having heeded his own advice: 'The eagle never lost so much time as when he submitted to learn of the crow.'

123
124
125
The critic John Ruskin (1819–1900) admired *The Horse*, another of the series; and so did Yeats. Dante Gabriel Rossetti (1828–82) praised the *Hermit's Dog* and *The Eagle*. ('When thou seest an Eagle, thou seest a portion of Genius; lift up thy head!')

The 'good Blake', always industrious, scarcely ever refused any work offered him, but he did refuse to paint hand-screens for Cowper's relation Lady Hesketh; and he did unburden his growing irritation in his notebook:

When H——y finds out what you cannot do,
That is the very thing he'll set you to.

But Blake's Angels had known what they were about when they sent him to his 'three years' Slumber on the banks of the Ocean' at Felpham. He had never before lived in the country. He and Catherine had loved to go on country rambles on the south side of the Thames, where, about Peckham Rye and neighbouring Kent villages, there were lanes, elms and harvest-fields. Now both sea and country lanes were at their door. We see Mrs Blake 'courting the embraces of Neptune'; and for Blake his six-roomed cottage was for a time – until growing irritation with his employer made his position intolerable – paradise. He wrote to Flaxman on his arrival:

'It is a perfect Model for Cottages &, I think, for Palaces of Magnificence, only Enlarging, not altering its proportions, & adding ornaments not principals. Nothing can be more Grand than its Simplicity & Usefulness. Simple without Intricacy, it seems to be the Spontaneous Effusion of Humanity, congenial to the wants of Man.'

126
That cottage is immortalized in one of the pages of *Milton*, the poem he wrote at Felpham. We see the poet walking in his garden while one of the 'daughters of inspiration' descends towards him from the tops of some neighbouring trees.

Blake was overwhelmed by the glory of nature; but characteristically, neither then nor at any time did he see nature as other than human; and the visionary experience

126 Blake's cottage at Felpham, from *Milton: A Poem*, c. 1804–8.

Famish'd, weeping, weak
With hollow piteous shriek

Rising from unrest,
The trembling woman prest,
With feet of weary woe;
She could no further go.

In his arms he bore,
Her arm'd with sorrow sore:
Till before their way,
A couching lion lay.

Turning back was vain,
Soon his heavy mane,
Bore them to the ground,
Then he stalk'd around.

Smelling to his prey,
But their fears allay,
When he licks their hands:
And silent by them stands.

They look upon his eyes
Fill'd with deep surprise:
And wondering behold,
A spirit arm'd in gold.

On his head a crown
On his shoulders down,
Flow'd his golden hair,
Gone was all their care.

Follow me he said,
Weep not for the maid;
In my palace deep,
Lyca lies asleep.

Then they followed,
Where the vision led;
And saw their sleeping child,
Among tygers wild.

To this day they dwell
In a lonely dell
Nor fear the wolvish howl,
Nor the lions growl.

here described culminated in an epiphany of the Grand Man
of the heavens:

My Eyes more & more
Like a Sea without Shore
Continue Expanding,
The Heavens commanding,
Till the Jewels of Light,
Heavenly Men beaming Bright,
Appear'd as One Man
Who Complacent began
My limbs to infold
In his beams of bright gold;
Like dross purg'd away
All my mire & my clay.

This vision of the spiritual sun is gloriously illustrated in Plate
47 of *Milton*, and described in that poem in mythological terms
as an encounter with Los, the Apollo of Blake's spiritual world.

Blake never depicted or described the least flower or tiniest
insect but some fairy or small spirit of life inhabited it; 'for
everything is human! mighty! sublime!' Nor was he above
seeing (and drawing) fairies. These he regarded as the living
spirits of the vegetable world, belonging to nature, and as such
mortal. An episode is recorded by Allan Cunningham in his
short memoir of Blake (1830): '"Did you ever see a fairy's funeral,
madam?" he once said to a lady who happened to sit by him in
company. "Never, sir," was the answer. "I have!" said Blake, "but
not before last night. I was walking alone in my garden; there
was great stillness among the branches and flowers, and more
than common sweetness in the air; I heard a low and pleasant
sound, and I knew not whence it came. At last, I saw the broad
leaf of a flower move, and underneath I saw a procession of
creatures of the size and colour of green and grey grasshoppers,
bearing a body laid on a rose-leaf which they buried with songs,
and then disappeared. It was a fairy funeral."'

Blake was no more attracted to seascapes than to landscape
painting. But *The Waters prevailed upon the Earth* and other
paintings may indeed owe something to his four years'
neighbourhood with Neptune. His trees – or Tree, for it is
always the one Tree that he depicts, stylized according to its
good or its evil aspect – are depicted with minutely observed
natural detail, like the bole of the elm in 'The Little Girl Found';
and he had a preoccupation with roots, in which Samuel Palmer

127

127 *Songs of Experience*, 1789. 'The Little Girl Found'.

was to follow him. His skies and clouds, as rich in the radiance of their colouring as Turner's, are still to be seen in the ever-varying and beautiful gilded skies of London, the aspect of natural beauty most familiar to a child of city streets. One might call Blake a painter of sky-scapes; indeed almost every page of his illuminated books is luminous like a sky. Blake, like Turner, supremely admired the paintings of Claude. He later communicated this admiration to Samuel Palmer, pointing out to his young disciple 'that in these, when minutely examined, there were, upon the focal lights of the foliage, small specks of pure white which made them appear to be glittering with dew which the morning sun had not yet dried up.... His description of these genuine Claudes, I shall never forget. He warmed with his subject, and it continued through an evening walk. The sun was set; but Blake's Claudes made sunshine in that shady place.'

Blake admired Constable too. Examining some of his work, he exclaimed 'Why, this is vision'; to which the more prosaic Constable replied that he 'took it to be painting'.

By the beginning of 1802 Blake was restive at Felpham. He confided to Butts that 'When I came down here, I was more sanguine than I am at present.' While he was kept busy 'Engraving the small plates for a New Edition of Mr Hayley's Triumphs of Temper from drawings by Maria Flaxman, sister to my friend the Sculptor', he was contrasting in his heart the apparent kindness of Hayley with the real understanding of Thomas Butts. Even at Felpham, he found time to produce for Butts works which came (as he wrote in November 1802) 'from my Head & my Heart in Unison'. Of not one work done for Hayley could that truly be said.

The crisis came in an unexpected manner. In the summer of 1803 Blake found in the garden of his cottage a soldier, called in by the gardener, it seems, to cut the grass. Blake did not like soldiers; he was against war as such, and against the war of English intervention in France in particular. He ordered the intruder out, and when he protested, threw him out by main force. Ill-advised words followed – reported as 'Damn the King, and damn all his soldiers, they are all slaves' – and some remarks about Napoleon more fitted to the mouth of a French than of an English poet. On this occasion Hayley came to Blake's defence in fine style, and he was acquitted. No doubt he was innocent. Yet the words imputed to him were such as he might well have spoken in anger, and his Felpham neighbours

128, 129 Illustrations to William Cowper's poem, 'The Task', c. 1820–5. LEFT *Winter;* RIGHT *Evening.*

Spiritual Enemies

would have been aware of his political views; he was not the man to conceal them.

Blake was to continue to work for Hayley for a time after his return to London, and to write to him in a friendly manner.

The works done for Butts at Felpham are listed in Blake's letters. They include the *Riposo* (*The Holy Family in Egypt*) which Blake considered his best picture 'in many respects'. He wrote to Butts in July 1803 that: 'I have now on the Stocks the following drawings for you: 1. Jephthah sacrificing his Daughter; 2. Ruth & her mother in Law & Sister; 3. The Three Maries at the Sepulcher; 4. The Death of Joseph; 5. The Death of the Virgin Mary; 6. St Paul Preaching; & 7. The Angel of the Divine Presence clothing Adam & Eve with Coats of Skins.

'These are all in great forwardness, & I am satisfied that I improve very much & shall continue to do so while I live, which is a blessing I can never be too thankful for both to God & Man.' The drawings numbered 5 and 7 are indeed among Blake's finest works.

Blake had also been working for other 'masters': 'But none can know the Spiritual Acts of my three years' Slumber on the banks of the Ocean, unless he has seen them in the Spirit, or unless he should read My long Poem descriptive of those Acts; for I have in these three years composed an immense number of verses in One Grand Theme, Similar to Homer's Iliad or Milton's Paradise Lost, the Persons & Machinery entirely new to the Inhabitants of Earth (some of the Persons Excepted). I have written this Poem from immediate Dictation, twelve or sometimes twenty or thirty lines at a time, without Premeditation & even against my Will; the Time it has taken in writing was thus render'd Non Existent, & an immense Poem Exists which seems to be the Labour of a long Life, all produc'd without Labour or Study. I mention this to show what I think the Grand Reason of my being brought down here.'

The poem *Milton* was, of course, the labour of a long life: Blake's own. His immense reading, his impassioned thought on the poetic and moral issues of which he treats, his continuous observation of man and nature, bore fruit. He himself was the Mental Traveller in land of imagination, where:

... the Babe is born in joy
That was begotten in dire woe;
Just as we Reap in Joy the fruit
Which we in bitter tears did sow.

As with Coleridge (whose *Kubla Khan* no opium could have evoked, had his mind and imagination been less richly stored with his readings in philosophy, poetry and unnumbered books), Blake's effortless composition of his great poem was the reward of year-long labours.

The theme of *Milton* is poetic inspiration as a way of redemption from the tyrannous law of 'Satan, the Selfhood', framer of 'natural religion', the maker of moral laws. I have read this poem many times; and while there may be greater themes attempted in *Jerusalem, Milton* is of all Blake's longer poems the most delightful. The influence of Felpham's natural beauty is to be sensed in the exquisite passages on flowers, insects, trees and birds; and there are passages of sustained eloquence equal to Milton himself.

The plates of *Milton* are not on the whole so magnificent as those of *Jerusalem*, but two or three are very fine. On Plate 18, the poet pulls down the familiar figure of Urizen (Satan) with his Tables of the Law. Plate 16 illustrates the 'inspired man', a Michelangelesque nude, casting off 'the rotten rags of memory' in 'the grandeur of inspiration'. On Plate 42 an eagle, somewhat resembling the one Blake designed for Hayley, hovers over two sleeping figures on a sea-washed rock. Plates 32 and 37 are identical, but in reverse: one shows William, in the light of day, with a star or comet falling to his foot; on the reverse plate, Robert, in the mystery of the night, is William's counterpart. It is implied, perhaps, that Robert is one of the 'authors in eternity' who dictated the poem to his mortal brother.

The etching of the plates was no doubt done after Blake's return to London, at the end of 1803 – and perhaps some of the

130 *Milton, c.* 1804–8. Plate 18.

131 *The Temptation and Fall of Eve*, from *Paradise Lost*, 1808.
132 *Satan watching the Caresses of Adam and Eve*, from *Paradise Lost*, 1808.
The finished version.

composition also; the title-page is dated 1804, but none of the three copies known to exist was printed before 1808.

Blake's relationship to Milton – lifelong and intimate – was at once one of admiration of the poet who was for him type and exemplar of 'the inspired man', and disagreement with the Puritan theologian. In *The Marriage of Heaven and Hell* (1790–3) Blake had already defined the ground of his disagreement – Milton had allowed the demon Reason to curb the energy of his Desire: 'Those who restrain desire do so because theirs is weak enough to be restrained; and the restrainer or reason usurps its place & governs the unwilling.... The history of this is written in Paradise Lost, & the Governor or Reason is call'd Messiah.' But 'this history has been adopted by both parties. It indeed appear'd to Reason as if Desire was cast out; but the Devil's account is, that the Messiah fell & form'd a heaven of what he stole from the Abyss.'

This usurpation, and the building of the Hell of the 'ratio of the five senses' is the theme of *Milton.* By exposing the deceiver, the poet Blake undertook to release the poet Milton (type of the 'inspired man') from the bondage of rationalism; the mind of the human ego, or 'selfhood', as Blake termed it. Long after, in 1825, he told the diarist Crabb Robinson:

'I saw Milton in imagination, and he told me to beware of being misled by his *Paradise Lost.* In particular he wished me to shew the falsehood of his doctrine that the pleasure of sex arose from the Fall. The Fall could not produce any pleasure.'

Darrell Figgis (editor of *Paintings of William Blake*, 1925) thought that the first of Blake's designs for Milton's poems was the single separate drawing entitled *Satan watching the Endearments of Adam and Eve.* 'He floats, wingless, above the endearments of the pair. He holds his head in his hands, and looks with horror on the "pleasures of sex", here found in exercise before the Fall.'

Of the two sets of watercolour drawings for *Comus* which Blake made, one must date from the Felpham period, for Blake wrote to Flaxman in 1801 that a friend – 'Mr Thomas' – had commissioned a set of designs, to be sent care of Flaxman. Neither set is dated.

Blake was to make his first series of drawings for *Paradise Lost* soon after the completion of his own poem, *Milton*, in 1807. In the following year he made another and finer series for Butts. In both, the original idea of the pleasure of sex existing before the Fall is retained. Blake had written, in *The Marriage of Heaven and Hell*, that 'the original Archangel, or possessor of the command of the heavenly host, is call'd the Devil or Satan, and his children are call'd Sin & Death. But in the Book of Job,

34-6

134-5

131-2

133 *Paradise Regained, c. 1816–18. Christ Tempted by Satan to turn the Stones to Bread.*

Milton's Messiah is call'd Satan.' The illustrations to *L'Allegro* and *Il Penseroso* (1816) were probably the last works Butts bought from Blake. Those to *L'Allegro* include the 'spiritual form' of the lark, which in the poem *Milton* is Blake's symbol of poetic inspiration, soaring towards Milton's 'watch-towre in the skies'.

136-7 The illustrations to the *Hymn on the Morning of Christ's Nativity*, which include the beautiful *Descent of Peace*, belong to an earlier period, about 1809.

133, 138 The series of twelve drawings for *Paradise Regained* belonged to John Linnell (1792–1882), the younger artist who befriended Blake in his last years (see p. 183), which suggests that they were made at about the same time as the *L'Allegro* and *Il Penseroso*. Blake's identification of Satan with the worldly wisdom of human reason and the moral law is brought out clearly. Satan, 138 in *Christ's Troubled Sleep*, is the same figure of Urizen who, 50 on the title-page of *Visions of the Daughters of Albion*, pursues Oothoon, Blake's eloquent pleader for sexual freedom. In his 130 *Milton* the poet (Plate 18) is shown pulling down the image of the same figure. *Christ's Troubled Sleep*, as Darrell Figgis points out, is a foreshadowing of the more terrible vision of *Job* (Plate 11):

134 *The Magic Banquet with the Lady Spell-bound*, from *Comus*, c. 1801.
135 *Comus and his Levellers*, c. 1801.

Spiritual Enemies

'With Dreams upon my bed thou searest me & affrightest me with Visions.'

Here we see 'Milton's Messiah' as the impostor whose cloven foot reveals his true nature. From first to last Blake was consistent in his affirmation that the God of Deism – 'Natural Religion' – is the Satan of the Prophets and of the Everlasting Gospel of 'Jesus, the Imagination'.

The sacrifice of his integrity as an artist for profit was for Blake an impossibility. During the years with Hayley he tried to silence his conscience in obedience to the good advice of his 'natural friends'. To begin with he had endeavoured 'with my whole might' to 'chain my feet to the world of Duty & Reality; but in vain! The faster I bind, the better is the Ballast, for I, so far from being bound down, take the world with me in my flights & often it seems lighter than a Ball of wool rolled by the wind.... Alas! wretched, happy, ineffectual labourer of time's moments that I am! Who shall deliver me from this spirit of Abstraction & Improvidence?'

But Blake knew at heart that the voice that urged him to obey 'Duty and Reality' in order to make money was the voice of the Devil. Six months after his arrival in Felpham, in January 1802, he was confiding to Butts that the Inspirers would not let him escape from them: 'I am under the direction of Messengers from Heaven, Daily & Nightly; but the nature of such things is not, as some suppose, without trouble or care. Temptations are on the right hand & left; behind, the sea of time & space roars & follows swiftly; he who keeps not right onwards is lost, & if our footsteps slide in clay, how can we do otherwise than fear & tremble?.... But if we fear to do the dictates of our Angels, & tremble at the Tasks set before us; if we refuse to do Spiritual Acts because of Natural Fears or Natural Desires! Who can describe the dismal torments of such a state!'

And finally – no myth or metaphor this time – Blake made his decision, heroic under the circumstances (the letter, again, is to Butts):

'And now, My Dear Sir, Congratulate me on my return to London, with the full approbation of Mr Hayley & with Promise – But, Alas!

'Now I may say to you, what perhaps I should not dare to say to anyone else: That I can alone carry on my visionary studies in London unannoy'd, & that I may converse with my friends in Eternity, See Visions, Dream Dreams & prophecy

136 From *Hymn on the Morning of Christ's Nativity*, c. 1814–16. 'The Annunciation to the Shepherds.'
137 From *Hymn on the Morning of Christ's Nativity*, c. 1814–16. 'The Descent of Peace.'

138 *Paradise Regained*, c. 1816–18. 'Christ's Troubled Sleep.'

& speak Parables unobserv'd & at liberty from the Doubts of other Mortals; perhaps Doubts proceeding from Kindness, but Doubts are always pernicious, Especially when we Doubt our Friends. Christ is very decided on this Point; "He who is Not With Me is Against Me." There is no Medium or Middle state; & if a Man is the Enemy of my Spiritual Life while he pretends to be the Friend of my Corporeal, he is a Real Enemy....'

Chapter 9
Visions of Albion

Blake returned to London from Felpham at the age of forty-five, and in the years that followed was to turn material defeat into spiritual victory. As he later confided to his Notebook, the Devil holds the money bag; but he faced adversity industriously and cheerfully:

I have Mental Joy & Mental Health
And Mental Friends & Mental wealth;
I've a Wife I love & that loves me;
I've all But Riches Bodily.
I am in God's presence night & day,
And he never turns his face away.
The accuser of sins by my side does stand
And he holds my money bag in his hand.

Blake made, not for Lambeth, but for his native district, and took a lease on the first floor at No. 17 South Molton Street. This was to be his home for nearly seventeen years. Not a house, this time, or even a six-roomed cottage. He had come down in the world; but his wants were few, and his childlessness, in the circumstances, was fortunate for his art and his visions. And in a spirit of renewed hope he engraved the magnificent title-page of a new poem: *Jerusalem: The Emanation of the Giant Albion* (1804).

139   It is impossible to know whether Blake had already begun the poem at Felpham, and, if so, how much was written there. But as surely as *Milton* breathes the atmosphere of the paradisal cottage, *Jerusalem* reflects the sombre grandeur of London:

In Felpham I heard and saw the Visions of Albion
I write in South Molton Street what I both see and hear
In regions of Humanity, in London's opening streets.

139 *Jerusalem*, 1804–20. Title-page. The soul's metamorphosis is here completed in the beautiful winged figure of Jerusalem.

This great poem, with its superb engraved pages, was to be Blake's companion over many years. It seems likely that he designed the title-page while very little of the poem yet existed in visible form. Southey is said to have seen part of it in 1811: 'a perfectly mad poem called Jerusalem'. None of the five copies printed by Blake is on paper watermarked earlier than 1818, and Keynes believes that Blake continued to add to the poem until 1820. He illuminated only one copy. This is probably the one to which he refers in a letter to George Cumberland written in 1827: 'The Last Work I produced is a Poem entitled Jerusalem the Emanation of the Giant Albion, but find that to Print it will Cost my time the amount of Twenty Guineas. One I have Finish'd. It contains 100 Plates but it is not likely that I shall get a Customer for it.'

He did not. This glorious book passed into the hands of Frederick Tatham after Catherine Blake's death. There are a few other illuminated pages of great beauty, evidently from another projected copy as different in colour and spirit as one copy of *Songs of Innocence* is from another.

As a poem, it is not so much a work of that 'hammered gold and gold enamelling' in which Blake's greatest disciple Yeats tempered his style, as a gold-mine. Blake's 'visions' do not belong to time, but to the timeless; they are related as parts to a whole, but as parts of the surface of a sphere, all equidistant from the centre, rather than in the time sequence to which in this world we are normally confined. Like dreams, they came to him in single symbolic episodes, or images; there is some attempt at chronology, but the material does not lend itself to

140 *Jerusalem*, 1804–20. Plate 18: Vala, Jerusalem and their children reconciled.

141 *Jerusalem*, 1804–20. Plate 53: Vala on a sunflower. The figure resembles Indian deities depicted in Edward Moor's *Hindu Pantheon* (1810), and is an instance of Blake's interest in 'the religions of all nations' as an expression of the one Imagination.
142 *Jerusalem*, 1804–20. Plate 28. Detail of a proof impression, c. 1820.

this order, any more than would a series of vivid dreams, all relating, perhaps, to an unfolding situation, but not forming a consecutive narrative. Blake added to *Jerusalem* over many years, inserting passages which may be fine in themselves but which further destroyed the continuity.

Visually, every page is beautiful and some are magnificent. The proportion of decoration to script is as perfect as in the *Songs.* There could be no greater contrast than between these lovingly composed pages, and the ill-proportioned pages of Young's *Night Thoughts*, or even the over-large pages of Gray. A single inspiration informs words and decoration alike.

Some of the themes are, nevertheless, extremely obscure. Is the swan-headed maiden on Plate 11 Finola, daughter of Lir, changed into a swan by her stepmother, or Sabrina, named on the text of the page? Who are the man-headed horses who draw the plough on Plate 29? What is the serpent-wheeled chariot of Plate 41? Whose is the terrible face, which seems to belong to the Expressionist art of a century later, surrounded by what appear to be peacock-feathers?

The pages of *Jerusalem* are Blake at his most Blakean. The figures are executed in his fully evolved and simplified linear style, that outline without volume which Roger Fry disliked but which is perfectly adapted to the novel technique Blake had invented. The linear decoration is itself calligraphic, merging harmoniously with the script. Grand, grotesque or lovely forms depict, as in some visual Divine Comedy, inner states of soul.

Blake can be horrific, but he is never, like his friend Fuseli, obscene; he never incites to evil by presenting it as alluring, but describes it, in the spirit of Dante, with prophetic purity.

In *Jerusalem* the reduction of Michelangelesque forms to linear terms is complete. It is the style of Blake's creation, fully realized in its own terms, and in Plate 97 for example, pointing forward to such artists as Rouault. Many like Plate 32, *Vala and Jerusalem*, and Plate 99, *The Union of the Soul with God*, are superb; all the old flow of vital energy is there, but with a new grandeur and maturity of vision. As Anthony Blunt wrote: 'Innocence is impossible to recapture, but here the artist has expressed the final state to which man can aspire by means of love and imagination after passing through the dark stage of Experience.'

Several of the separate plates are more highly finished than those which combine text and decoration, for instance the Frontispiece, in which Man enters by a dark door into the 'regions of the grave' of earthly life, and the flame-enveloped figure (Orc?) of Plate 26. The depiction of Albion before Jesus,

143 *Jerusalem*, 1804–20. Plate 62.

Repose on me till the morning of the Grave. I am thy life.
Jerusalem replied. I am an outcast: Albion is dead.
I am left to the trampling foot & the spurning heel.
A Harlot I am call'd. I am sold from street to street.
I am defaced with blows & with the dirt of the Prison.
And wilt thou become my Husband O my Lord & Saviour?
Shall Vala bring thee forth? shall the Chaste be ashamed also?
I see the Maternal Line, I behold the Seed of the Woman.
Cainah, & Ada & Zillah & Naamah Wife of Noah.
Shuahs daughter & Tamar & Rahab the Canaanites:
Ruth the Moabite & Bathsheba of the daughters of Heth
Naamah the Ammonite, Zibeah the Philistine. & Mary
These are the Daughters of Vala, Mother of the Body of death
But I thy Magdalen behold thy Spiritual Risen Body
Shall Albion arise? I know he shall arise at the Last Day?
I know that in my flesh I shall see God: but Emanations
Are weak. they know not whence they are, nor whither tend.

Jesus replied. I am the Resurrection & the Life.
I Die & pass the limits of possibility, as it appears
To individual perception. Luvah must be Created
And Vala: for I cannot leave them in the gnawing Grave.
But will prepare a way for my banished-ones to return
Come now with me into the villages. walk thro all the cities.
Tho thou art taken to prison & judgement, starved in the streets
I will command the cloud to give thee food & the hard rock
To flow with milk & wine, tho thou seest me not a season
Even a long season & a hard journey & a howling wilderness.
Tho Valas cloud hide thee & Luvahs fires follow thee:
Only believe & trust in me, Lo. I am always with thee.

So spake the Lamb of God while Luvahs Cloud reddening above
Burst forth in streams of blood upon the heavens & dark night
Involved Jerusalem. & the Wheels of Albions Sons turnd hoarse
Over the Mountains & the fires blaz'd on Druid Altars
And the Sun set in Tyburns Brook where Victims howl & cry.

But Los beheld the Divine Vision among the flames of the Furnaces
Therefore he lived & breathed in hope. but his tears fell incessant
Because his Children were closd from him apart: & Enitharmon
Dividing in fierce pain: also the Vision of God was clos'd in clouds
Of Albions Spectres, that Los in despair oft sat, & often pondered
On Death Eternal in fierce shudders upon the mountains of Albion
Walking: & in the vales in howlings fierce, then to his Anvils
turning, anew began his labours, tho in terrible pains.

Awake! Awake Jerusalem! O lovely Emanation of Albion
Awake and overspread all Nations as in Ancient Time
For lo! the Night of Death is past and the Eternal Day
Appears upon our Hills: Awake Jerusalem and come away

So spake the Vision of Albion & in him so spake in my hearing
The Universal Father. Then Albion stretch'd his hand into Infinitude.
And took his Bow. Fourfold the Vision for bright beaming Urizen
Layd his hand on the South. & took a breathing Bow of carved Gold
Luvah his hand stretch'd to the East & bore a Silver Bow bright shining
Tharmas Westward a Bow of Brass pure flaming richly wrought
Urthona Northward in thick storms a Bow of Iron terrible thundering

And the Bow is a Male & Female & the Quiver of the Arrows of Love
Are the Children of his Bow: a Bow of Mercy & Loving-kindness: laying
Open the hidden Heart in Wars of mutual Benevolence Wars of Love
And the Hand of Man grasps firm between the Male & Female Loves
And he Clothed himself in Bow & Arrows in awful state Fourfold
In the midst of his Twenty-eight Cities each with his Bow breathing

The handwritten text on the plate:

Leaning against the pillars, & his disease rose from his skirts
Upon the Precipice he stood ready to fall into Non-Entity.
Los was all astonishment & terror: he trembled sitting on the Stone
Of London: but the interiors of Albions fibres & nerves were hidden
From Los; astonishd he beheld only the petrified surfaces:
And saw his Furnaces in ruins, for Los is the Demon of the Furnaces;
He saw also the Four Points of Albion reversd inwards
He siezd his Hammer & Tongs, his iron Poker & his Bellows,
Upon the valleys of Middlesex, Shouting loud for aid Divine.

In stern defiance came from Albions bosom, Hand, Hyle, Koban,
Gwantok, Peachy, Brertun, Slaid, Huttn, Skofeld, Kock, Kotype,
Bowen, Albions Sons: they bore him a golden couch into the porch
And on the Couch reposd his limbs trembling from the bloody field.
Rearing their Druid Patriarchal rocky Temples around his limbs.
(All things begin & end, in Albions Ancient Druid Rocky Shore.)

144 *Jerusalem*, 1804–20. Plate 97: Los.
145 *Jerusalem*, 1804–20. Plate 32. Vala is the tutelary spirit of St Paul's; Jerusalem, the soul, and bride of Jesus, of Westminster Abbey and spiritual religion.

All Human Forms identified even Tree Metal Earth & Stone, all
Human Forms identified, living going forth & returning wearied
Into the Planetary lives of Years Months Days & Hours reposing
And then Awaking into his Bosom in the Life of Immortality.
And I heard the Name of their Emanations they are named Jerusalem

The End of The Song
of Jerusalem

146 *Jerusalem*, 1804–20. Plate 99: 'The Union of the Soul with God.'
147 *Jerusalem*, 1804–20. Plate 76: 'Albion worshipping Christ.'

By Satans Watch-fiends tho they search numbering every grain
Of sand on Earth every night, they never find this Gate.
It is the Gate of Los. Withoutside is the Mill, intricate, dreadful.
And filld with cruel tortures; but no mortal man can find the Mill
Of Satan, in his mortal pilgrimage of seventy years.
  For Human beauty knows it not: nor can Mercy find it! But
In the Fourth region of Humanity, Urthona named
Mortality begins to roll the billows of Eternal Death
Before the Gate of Los. Urthona here is named Los.
And here begins the System of Moral Virtue, named Rahab.
Albion fled thro' the Gate of Los, and he stood in the Gate.

Los was the friend of Albion who most lovd him. In Cambridgeshire
His eternal station, he is the twenty-eighth, & is four-fold.
Seeing Albion had turnd his back against the Divine Vision,
Los said to Albion, Whither fleest thou? Albion replyd.

I die! I go to Eternal Death! the shades of death
Hover within me & beneath, and spreading themselves outside
Like rocky clouds, build me a gloomy monument of woe:
Will none accompany me in my death? or be a Ransom for me
In that dark Valley? I have girded round my cloke, and on my feet
Bound these black shoes of death, & on my hands, deaths iron gloves
God hath forsaken me. & my friends are become a burden
A weariness to me, & the human footstep is a terror to me.

Los answerd, troubled: and his soul was rent in twain:
Must the Wise die for an Atonement? does Mercy endure Atonement?
No! It is Moral Severity, & destroys Mercy in its Victim.
So speaking not yet infected with the Error & Illusion

147   crucified upon the Tree of Life (Plate 76), is the most moving
depiction of the relationship between the mortal and the divine
humanity known to me. It has the completeness of an icon, in
which there is nothing superfluous and nothing lacking.

During the years in South Molton Street, *Jerusalem* was
Blake's life, but not his livelihood. When he left Felpham it
was understood that he was to continue to work for Hayley,
and there was much correspondence on the plates of the *Life
of Romney* which was to follow Cowper's *Life*. (Only one of the
plates in the life of Cowper was, in the end, both designed and
engraved by Blake; five more were engraved after other artists.)
Flaxman wrote to Hayley saying that he had seen 'two or three
noble sketches by Blake', and offering to see to it that Blake's
engraving of these should fit in with the other designs. But
all this came to nothing; Hayley employed Caroline Watson
(*c*. 1761–1814) instead of Blake, who was gradually ousted from
the project. Blake finally engraved only one of the eleven plates,
after Romney; the portrait of Romney which he drew and
engraved was not used.

For all his industry, Blake again and again found himself
in a similar situation; and at a certain point, a reputation for
failure becomes self-perpetuating.

Meanwhile, an apparently more promising project was in
the air. In 1805, two years after Blake's return to London, an
engraver turned publisher named Cromeck commissioned
him to make a series of designs for Blair's *Grave*, on the
149   understanding that Blake should also be the engraver. A list
of subscribers was opened, the reputation of Blake being the
main attraction. Fuseli, always a faithful friend, wrote the
foreword. The list of subscribers was long and contained many
names distinguished in the art world of the day. But once in his
hands, Cromeck gave the designs to the engraver Schiavonetti,
a pupil of the 'smooth' (to use Blake's word for him) Bartolozzi.
Blake was doubly enraged: at the spoiling of his work, and at
the financial loss. Gilchrist calculated that Cromeck made
about £1,800 from sales of the book, of which £500 went to
Schiavonetti and only £20 to Blake.

Still worse, seeing Blake at work on his composition of *The
150   Canterbury Pilgrims*, Cromeck went to Blake's old acquaintance
Stothard and proposed the subject to him as an original idea
of his own, without mentioning that Blake was working on it.
Cromeck in due course published an engraving from Stothard's
painting, at great profit to himself. Blake's long friendship with

148 *Jerusalem*, 1804–20. Plate 39.

Stothard was broken with much indignation on both sides, and again he was cheated of hope of financial reward for his work.

In desperation Blake arranged an exhibition in his brother's shop at 28 Broad Street, and there in 1809 his own *Canterbury Pilgrims* (a 'fresco') was shown together with fifteen other paintings. The prospectus advertised Blake's intention to make an engraving, and invited subscriptions. But Blake was no match for the Cromecks of this world; few visited the obscure exhibition, and only three or four copies of the *Descriptive Catalogue* now exist. Among those who did see the exhibition were the diarist Crabb Robinson and the essayist Charles Lamb (an admirer of Blake's poems, as also was Coleridge). To Lamb's credit, he preferred Blake's *Canterbury Pilgrims* to Stothard's, calling it 'A work of wonderful power and spirit, hard and dry, yet with grace.' He was also delighted by the *Descriptive Catalogue*, declaring that Blake's analysis of the characters in Chaucer's 'Prologue' was the finest criticism of that poem he had ever read. Southey, hostile as ever, described Blake's (now lost) painting of the *Ancient Britons* as 'one of his worst pictures, which is saying much'. This was the work which attracted most attention at the time; Lamb mentions it in his account of the exhibition.

Needless to say, Blake found few subscribers for his engraving. The tempera was bought by the faithful Butts. The bitterest irony in the story of Blake's failures and humiliations is that he was never unknown; on the contrary, he was in the heart of London's art world, and knew all the most famous artists and engravers of his day. And yet he failed where they succeeded, ousted by men of inferior talents and passed over by lifelong friends.

Jacob Bronowski saw economics as a cause of Blake's failure: he points to the decline of the craft of copper-plate engraving as cheaper methods of reproduction were invented. But David Erdman probably comes nearer to the truth in seeing the question as being, rather, why should Blake have failed where others – Stothard, Bartolozzi, Schiavonetti and the rest – succeeded? His genius was of a magnitude, and of a nature, to call in question too many accepted values. He was the Samson predestined to pull down a civilization founded upon the accepted ideas, verities and platitudes of his day. Against the really new the passive resistance of every society is mustered; and Blake's (or Swedenborg's) New Age is even now still only in its birth-pangs.

It is hard enough that Blake, in 1814, was engraving, not his own, but Flaxman's designs for *Hesiod*; but to picture him – he must have been working at the time on some of his finest

The Counsellor, King, Warrior, Mother & Child, in the Tomb

149 Illustration to Robert Blair's *The Grave*, 1808, designed by Blake but engraved by Luigi Schiavonetti. *The Counsellor, King, Warrior, Mother and Child in the Tomb*.
150 Chaucer's *Canterbury Pilgrims*, 1810–20. Blake wrote: 'This Print is the Finest that has been done or is likely to be done in England'.

Visions of Albion

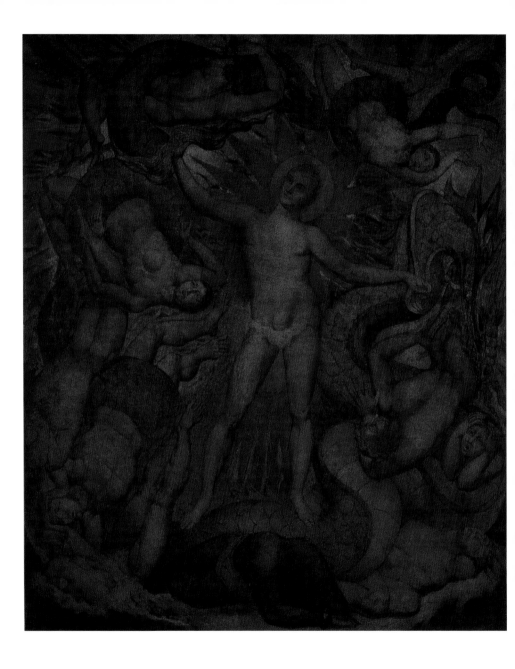

151 *The Spiritual Form of Nelson Guiding Leviathan, in whose wreathings are enfolded the Nations of the Earth.* Exhibited 1809.
152 *Laocoön,* 1815, for an article in Rees' *Cyclopaedia.*

This drawing was made by Mr Blake in the Royal
Academy Somerset House for a small plate he made of the
Laocoön for the Article in the Encyclopedia, the Article itself was
on Sculpture being written by Flaxman, when Mr B was drawing
his old friend Fuseli above in Said...

designs, the series of *L'Allegro* and *Il Penseroso* commissioned, need it be said, by Butts – thankful to execute soup-tureens for the Wedgwood catalogues, is almost unbearable. Another piece of hackwork was the engraving of some plates for Abraham Rees' *Cyclopedia* (1819). An example of sculpture selected by Flaxman (author of the article) was the Laocoon, which took the fifty-seven-year-old Blake to the Royal Academy's Antique School to make a drawing of the cast. His famous *Laocoön* engraving was the enduring outcome of this revisiting of an old haunt. 'What! you here, Meesther Blake?' said Keeper Fuseli; 'we ought to come and learn from you, not you from us.' Tatham, who records the incident, adds that Blake took his place among the students with simple, cheerful joy in his work.

Chapter 10
The Interpreter

For the six years following the 1809 exhibition at Broad Street we have little trace of Blake. He lived on in obscurity in South Molton Street, ceaselessly engaged in writing and painting, even though he was selling few pictures. It must have been during this period that he wrote many of the poems that were burned by Frederick Tatham, Catherine Blake's executor, after the poet's death. Tatham truly admired Blake, and recalled, long after, his first walk in Blake's company, which was 'like walking with the Prophet Isaiah'. But he belonged to the 'Apostolic Church' of clergyman Edward Irving (1792–1834), and presumably found some of Blake's prophecies – Isaiah or no – incompatible with that narrower creed. Blake could perhaps no longer afford the copper plates for the engraving of these later manuscripts as illuminated books, for which purchasers were so few. But they were, he said, 'the delight and study of archangels'; 'published elsewhere, and beautifully bound'.

But from the summer of 1818 a new circle of friends began to gather about him. George Cumberland, though he lived in Bristol, did not forget Blake, and sent him a young artist, John Linnell (1792–1882), who was to become the friend and supporter of his declining years. Even as a young man, Linnell had that capacity to cope with the affairs of this world which Blake so notably lacked. At the time he met Blake he was working mainly as a portrait-painter, and asked Blake's help in the engraving of a portrait. Through Linnell, Blake later (1824) met Samuel Palmer (then aged nineteen), who more than any other was the inheritor of something of Blake's vision. Palmer was the moving spirit of a group of young painters of his own generation known as the Shoreham Ancients, so named because Samuel Palmer and his father lived at Shoreham, and because they were in total revolt against the aesthetics of 'the moderns' of their day,

153

desiring, like Blake himself, a return to the 'Everlasting Gospel' of art, the Platonic and Plotinian philosophy of ideal form and ideal beauty. George Richmond (1809–96), later to become a fashionable portrait-painter, Edward Calvert (1799–1883, the oldest member of the group), supreme among engravers, F. O. Finch (1802–62), a watercolour painter, and the Tatham brothers, painter and architect, met weekly to discuss their work, and frequented Shoreham, Palmer's 'valley of vision', where Blake himself was a guest on at least one occasion. Linnell was a little older than these young enthusiasts (and not strictly one of the Shoreham group), but had early befriended Palmer, who later became his son-in-law.

Another group of new friends of an older generation were John Varley (1778–1842), a landscape painter, and the watercolourists Henry James Richter (1772–1857) and James Holmes (1777–1860). These forerunners and founders of the new English watercolour school Blake used to meet frequently at John Varley's house in Titchfield Street, within easy walking distance of South Molton Street. From them he learned (so his biographer Gilchrist thinks) 'to add greater fullness and depth of colour to his drawings'. Linnell had been Varley's pupil and it was he, presumably, who introduced Varley to Blake, soon after his meeting with him, in 1818.

At last, in Varley, Blake had a friend who did not consider his visions 'mad'. Varley was an astrologer, and apparently a highly professional and successful one. Sceptical Gilchrist admits that his predictions were astonishingly accurate. He was evidently also a student of other esoteric subjects, and it was under his encouragement and in his company that Blake was encouraged to draw (in a light-hearted spirit, as it seems) those strange 'spirit heads', authentic sketches of some of his spiritual visitants. One is again reminded of Swedenborg, who conversed with spirits of the departed almost as an everyday matter. These drawings – less imaginatively inspired, be it said, than Blake's more serious work – have a more-than-lifelike quality which bears witness, at least, to his astonishing power of visual fantasy. These heads illustrate his own assertion that 'He who does not imagine in stronger and better lineaments, and in stronger and better light than his perishing and mortal eye can see, does not imagine at all. The painter of this work asserts that all his imaginations appear to him infinitely more perfect and more minutely organized than any thing seen by his mortal eye. Spirits are organized men.'

154

153 Portrait of Blake by John Linnell, 1820.

Portrait of
John Blake 1820

J. L. [...]

The Interpreter

The forms these beings take often seems to derive from Blake's Gothic studies; many of the drawings are of kings and queens: Wallace and Edward the First, and other historical personages, vividly characterized. The ghost of a flea is one horribly memorable bloodthirsty demon. Linnell made a copy of Blake's drawing of this monster (and other of Blake's 'visions') for *Zodiacal Physiognomy*, as a type of the sign of Gemini. Allan Cunningham remembered how Varley (who probably believed in Blake's visions in a more literal sense than did Blake himself) described the conception of that 'naked figure with a strong body and a short neck – with burning eyes which long for moisture, and a face worthy of a murderer, holding a bloody cup in its clawed hands, out of which it seems eager to drink. I never saw any shape so strange, nor did I ever see any colouring so curiously splendid – a kind of glistening green and dusky gold, beautifully varnished. "But what in the world is it?" "It is a ghost, sir, – the ghost of a flea – a spiritualization of the thing!" "He saw this in a vision then," I said. "I'll tell you all about it, sir. I called on him one evening, and found Blake more than usually excited. He told me he

155-6

154 *The Man who taught Blake Painting in his Dreams*. Spirit head drawn for John Varley, c. 1825.

155 *The Head of a Ghost of a Flea*, c. 1819.

had seen a wonderful thing – the ghost of a flea! 'And did you make a drawing of him?' I inquired. 'No, indeed,' said he, 'I wish I had, but I shall, if he appears again!' He looked earnestly into a corner of the room, and said, 'there he is – reach me my things – I shall keep my eye on him. There he comes! his eager tongue whisking out of his mouth, a cup in his hand to hold blood and covered with a scaly skin of gold and green;' – as he described him so he drew him.'"

Whatever the explanation of this faculty, it was part of the make-up of Blake's genius. Yet such visualizations seem not to have come from his supreme world of imagination, 'Eden', but from some intermediate realm, Yeats' *Hodos chameleontos*, peopled by shifting forms and images. These spirit heads have in an exaggerated degree a characteristic we find in all Blake's depictions: the 'stronger and better lineaments' of spiritual individuality. Sometimes, accustomed as we are to the reticences of the fleshly veil (altogether absent in Blake's faces and forms), the impact of this unveiled purity of character and expression is like a shock. There is none among the historical

The Interpreter

or Biblical personages whom he depicted whose face and form alike are not expressive, in this total sense, of the character proper to them.

Blake's interest in human character and human types is most clearly expressed in his *Canterbury Pilgrims* (see p. 178) and in the essay he wrote on it for his *Descriptive Catalogue*. Here his view of character has some affinity with the theory of astrology, which is a science concerned with the description and classification of types:

'The characters of Chaucer's Pilgrims are the characters which compose all ages and nations: as one age falls, another rises, different to mortal sight, but to immortals only the same; for we see the same characters repeated again and again, in animals, vegetables, minerals, and in men; nothing new occurs in identical existence; Accident ever varies, Substance can never suffer change nor decay.'

As with that other spiritualist poet Yeats (who had read all Balzac and in *A Vision* described with extraordinary insight human types in terms of his twenty-eight 'phases of the moon'), characterization is a strong and unexpected element in Blake's work as an artist. His poetry, by contrast, seems to relate purely to an archetypal world, in which 'character' has no place.

As often happens when there is some inner transformation or development, outer circumstances also changed. In this happier phase of his life Blake moved (in 1821) from South Molton Street to No. 3 Fountain Court, off the Strand, a house belonging to a brother-in-law. It was a 'quiet court' when Blake lived there, with a glimpse of the Thames. It seemed a squalid place to Crabb Robinson:

'He was at work, engraving, in a small bedroom – light, and looking out on a mean yard – everything in the room squalid and indicating poverty, except himself.... There was but one chair in the room, besides that on which he sat. On my putting my hand to it, I found that it would have fallen to pieces if I had lifted it. So, as if I had been a Sybarite, I said, with a smile, "Will you let me indulge myself?" and sat on the bed near him. During my short stay there was nothing in him that betrayed that he was aware of what to other persons might have been even offensive – not in his person, but in all about him.'

Even Crabb Robinson seems to have sensed the special atmosphere of the 'House of the Interpreter', as the Shoreham Ancients called that poor room (the reference is to Bunyan's *Pilgrim's Progress*). Samuel Palmer used to kiss the threshold when he visited him. Palmer recalls Blake as 'one of the very few who cannot be depressed by neglect, and to whose name rank and station could add no lustre. Moving apart, in a sphere above

156 *The Ghost of a Flea, c.* 1819–20.

The Interpreter

the attraction of worldly honours, he did not accept greatness but confer it. He ennobled poverty, and by his conversation and the influence of his genius, made two small rooms in Fountain Court more attractive than the threshold of princes.'

157–60   Most seminal of Blake's works, for his young disciples, was the series of seventeen woodcuts illustrating a school edition of the *Pastorals* of Virgil, edited by Dr Thornton (1768–1837), a physician and noted botanist, author of several elegantly illustrated quartos and folios on the Linnaean system of plant classification. (He was also a friend of Varley's, at whose house Blake probably met him.) These were Blake's only woodcuts. 'The rough, unconventional work of a mere prentice hand at wood-engraving' (according to Gilchrist), they have the energy and invention of great art, and recall Blake's lifelong love of Albrecht Dürer, whose *Melancholia* (inspiration likewise of Milton's *Il Penseroso*) was always beside his work-table.

Thornton's publishers ridiculed Blake's work. 'This man must do no more,' was their verdict, and the blocks were given to be re-cut by one of their regular hands. For once Blake had natural friends to thank that these lovely works were not altogether and forever ruined. At a dinner party, Thornton met several artists – Thomas Lawrence, James Ward, Linnell and others – who all expressed their admiration for Blake's work in general and the woodcuts in particular. The Doctor restored the designs with a defensive apology: 'The illustrations of this English Pastoral are by the famous BLAKE, the illustrator of Young's *Night Thoughts*, and Blair's *Grave*; who designed and engraved them himself. This is mentioned as they display less art than genius, and are much admired by some eminent painters.'

The publishers had already cut down sixteen of Blake's seventeen blocks to fit their pages; providentially in eight instances proofs remain of the unmutilated and beautiful originals. In these images of the Earthly Paradise are there perhaps glimpses of Shoreham as well as memories of Felpham? For Blake had visited Palmer there, and stayed in his house. These works were the inspiration of Calvert and Palmer, who both surpassed Blake in technique though not in conception.

Samuel Palmer, in 1824, recorded in his notebook that intense and new delight Blake's woodcuts had brought to the Shoreham circle:

'I sat down with Mr Blake's Thornton's *Virgil* woodcuts before me, thinking to give to their merits my feeble testimony. I happened first to think of their sentiment. They are visions of little dells, and nooks, and corners of Paradise; models of the exquisitest pitch of intense poetry. I thought of their light and shade, and looking upon them I found no word to describe it.

The Interpreter

159 Illustration for Thornton's *Virgil*, 1821. 'Blasted Trees and Flattened Crops.'
160 Drawing for Thornton's *Virgil*, 1820. 'Thenot.'

Intense depth, solemnity, and vivid brilliancy only coldly
and partially describe them. There is in all such a mystic and
dreamy glimmer as penetrates and kindles the inmost soul,
and gives complete and unreserved delight, unlike the gaudy
daylight of this world. They are like all that wonderful artist's
works the drawing aside of the fleshly curtain, and the glimpse
which all the most holy, studious saints and sages have enjoyed,
of that rest which remaineth to the people of God.'

Calvert and Wilson, Blake and Claude
Prepared a rest for the people of God,
Palmer's phrase, but after that
Confusion fell upon our thought.

So Yeats links the names of the Shoreham Ancients with that
of Claude, whom Blake himself had taught them to admire.

Chapter 11
King and Priest in his own Household

161-8   The commission for the twenty-two *Illustrations of the Book
of Job* came from Linnell, in 1821, when Blake was sixty-five.
Linnell had seen the series of watercolour drawings Blake
had made for Butts, and he commissioned a second series
for himself. He paid Blake £5 per plate which enabled him
to work on the engravings. These illustrations, and the later,
unfinished, *Dante* series, are Blake's enduring masterworks;
as familiar to us as Bach's B-minor Mass or Shakespeare's
King Lear, and equal in conception to these, or to any of those
Florentine paintings he so ardently admired. They are supreme
masterpieces of the engraver's art. The clean strokes create
skies brilliant as with Northern Lights; the very aspect of
God has been given that majestical whirlwind form, which
prompted Robert Frost's Eve to exclaim: 'It's God. / I'd know
him from Blake's picture anywhere.'

Had not Blake's patron Hayley been a foolish egoist, and his
friend Flaxman content to 'help' Blake by passing on hackwork,
might we not have had other works as great from a spirit whose
like is so seldom in 'the world of generation'? It is sad to reflect
that as Samuel Palmer's father-in-law, Linnell was as insensitive
to the younger man's genius as Hayley and Flaxman had been
to Blake's.

The engraving of the plates for the reduced drawings made
by Blake for Linnell occupied three years. The surrounding
decorations are sketchily indicated in only two or three of the
drawings, and were evidently conceived in terms of the engraved
designs. In them Blake frequently reverts to the Gothic style of
Songs of Innocence and of Experience, and incorporates lettering
into the designs with a mastery born of his lifelong practice of
combining text and design.

Our Father which art in Heaven · hallowed be thy Name

1

Thus did Job continually

There was a Man in the Land of Uz whose Name was Job. & that Man was perfect & upright

The Letter Killeth
The Spirit giveth Life

It is Spiritually Discerned

& one that feared God & eschewed Evil & there was born unto him Seven Sons & Three Daughters

WBlake inv & sculp

London. Published as the Act directs. March 8: 1828. by Will Blake N³ Fountain Court Strand.

161 *Job in Prosperity*, 1825. Plate 1: 'Thus did Job continually'.

King and Priest in his own Household

162 TOP *The Wrath of Elihu*, 1825–6. Plate 12: 'I am Young and ye are very Old'.
163 ABOVE LEFT *The Book of Job*, 1825. Plate 15: 'God Pointing out Behemoth... and Leviathan'.
164 ABOVE RIGHT *The Book of Job*, 1825. Plate 20: 'Job Recounting his Experiences to his Daughters'.

165 *Satan Smiting Job with Sore Boils*, c. 1826.

Blake's *Illustrations of the Book of Job* are more than an illustration of the Bible; they are in themselves a prophetic vision, a spiritual revelation, at once a personal testimony and replete with Blake's knowledge of Christian Cabbala, Neoplatonism, and the mystical theology of the Western Esoteric tradition as a whole. They are a complete statement of Blake's vision of man's spiritual drama. The true God is the 'God within', enthroned in every human soul; the 'divine humanity' whose lineaments are those of Job himself. 'Satan, the Selfhood' is permitted to tempt Job. It is this Selfhood who makes havoc of Job's world; and as Satan assumes power, so the interior vision darkens and the 'God within' falls into the 'deadly sleep' of spiritual amnesia (Plate 5). Satan's supreme deception (Blake had given expression to this realization in *Milton*) is his claim to be God; a god external to the soul, framer of the moral law based upon the natural order of 'one law for the lion and ox'. Job's three friends are clearly based upon

Blake's own Zoas: Tharmas (the sensual man), Luvah (the man of feeling), and Urizen (the reasoner). The beautiful figure of Elihu, who, in Plate 12, ushering the first light of dawn among the fading stars, causes Job to look up in hope, is evidently Los, the poetic imagination, who 'kept the divine vision in time of trouble'.

162

In Plate 20 the sorrows through which Job, enslaved by his own ego, has passed, vanish like a dream. Blake had himself passed through long years of darkness, and knew the truth: 'for tho' on Earth things seem Permanent, they are less permanent than a Shadow, as we all know too well'. The glorious nature-poetry of the Hebrew poem is expressed no less in those 'men seen afar', the Stars of the Morning, than in the splendid theriomorphic forms of Behemoth and Leviathan (Plate 15), greatest of all Blake's exultant depictions of 'evil, or energy' in serpent-form, whose 'life delights in life'.

164

163

The series begins and ends with a symbolic expression of Blake's belief that Christianity is 'the liberty both of body & mind to exercise the Divine Arts of Imagination, Imagination the real & eternal World of which this Vegetable Universe is but a faint shadow.... Let every Christian, as much as in him lies, engage himself openly & publicly before all the World in some Mental pursuit for the Building up of Jerusalem.' In the first plate, Job and all his family are 'worshipping God' under the Tree of Life, on which hang their musical instruments, as untouched as on a Calvinist Sabbath. In the last plate, each has taken his instrument, and all are playing and singing with that joyful and tireless industry in things of spirit which for Blake was the essence of Christianity. All bear their part in making the music of Heaven.

As in *A Vision of the Last Judgment*, many of the *Job* engravings are formalized in the manner of spiritual diagrams. One world opens from another: those 'four worlds', or regions of consciousness, of Blake's own symbolic thought, derived from the Jewish esoteric tradition of the Cabbala, and the similar fourfold cosmology of Neoplatonism.

The two preliminary sets of watercolour drawings are scarcely less beautiful than the finished work. The engravings are the greater work, for they unite with grandeur of conception the consummate craftsmanship which was the fruit of Blake's years of practice in the engraver's art. When he had completed the set, he added to each during the actual process of engraving a border reminiscent of his illuminated books, in which text and decoration are harmoniously combined. Angels and devils, insects and tendrils surround the designs, as though Blake was

166 TOP LEFT *The Book of Job*, 1825. Plate 3: 'Satan Bringing Destruction on the Sons and Daughters of Job'.

167 TOP RIGHT *The Book of Job*, 1825. Plate 6: 'Satan Smiting Job with Sore Boils'.

168 ABOVE *The Book of Job*, 1825. Plate 13: 'God Appearing in the Whirlwind'.

reluctant to relinquish each deeply considered and lovingly executed plate.

The *Job* series won Ruskin's admiration: 'It is of the highest rank in certain characters of imagination and expression; in the mode of obtaining certain effects of light.... In expressing conditions of glaring and flickering light, Blake is greater than Rembrandt.'

One would like to know why, and for whom, Blake, in 1821, painted his fine illustration of a Neoplatonic mythological treatise – Porphyry's *De Antro Nympharum* – which he had read with delight (in Thomas Taylor's translation) years before, and whose influence is evident in the Lambeth Books. The Arlington Court tempera is scarcely in Thomas Butts' vein; and after about 1810 Butts bought fewer pictures – no doubt his house was already filled from floor to ceiling. It is likely, too (as Darrell Figgis suggested), that Blake at this time, his pride wounded by the failure of so many projects begun in hope, would not have been easy to approach. When it was discovered in 1949 at Arlington Court in Devon the painting still bore the label of the picture-framer, Linnell's father, but this does not necessarily mean that it had belonged to either of the Linnells.

One would like to think it was painted for George Cumberland, friend both of Blake and Thomas Taylor, the translator of Porphyry. There is no evidence that this is so, though its discovery in the West Country supports the idea, since Cumberland lived in Bristol.

The work is a fine example of Blake's late style. As in the *Job* series, there is the suggestion of an interpenetration of worlds or modes of consciousness. Porphyry interprets the Homeric 'cave of the nymphs', scene of Odysseus' return to Ithaca, as sacred to the mysteries of generation. The incarnating souls 'descend' from a radiant world, and on the looms of the nymphs are woven into earthly bodies. The principal figures in the painting are Odysseus and the goddess Athene, the divine wisdom: a figure not unlike the Dante series Blake painted soon afterwards. The sleeping figure in the sun-chariot suggests the drowsy 'God within' of *Job* 5; the Platonic 'cave' of generation in which the nymphs with urns on their heads are standing suggests the 'cave' of *Job* 2 and 14. In both cases the 'cave' symbolizes, as for Plato, this world.

It seems likely that the tempera was painted shortly before the *Job* series. It also looks forward to the last series of designs Blake was to create, before his tireless industry and delight in his work diminished as his body failed him: the illustrations to Dante. He was at work on these literally on his death-bed.

169 *The Sea of Time and Place*, 1821. Illustration to Thomas Taylor's translation of Porphyry's *De Antro Nympharum*. The kneeling figure is Odysseus, in the act of throwing the girdle lent him back to the sea-goddess Leucothea. Pallas Athene stands behind him, pointing to the heavenly world from which souls 'descend' into generation, to be woven into the mortal garments by the nymphs of the Cave, working at their looms and shuttles. The Three Fates are in the water of the estuary opening into 'the sea of time and space', drawing yarn from a distaff held by the sea-god Phorcis. Atropos holds the shears. The figures with full and empty buckets illustrate a Platonic parable from the same work.

He made over one hundred drawings – many of them mere sketches – and seven engravings, possibly none of them completed, but none the less among his greatest works. 'What you call finished is not even begun,' he had exclaimed to Moser, defender of the 'high finish' of 'paltry blots and blurs'. So, conversely, we see in Blake's beginnings the great conceptions of the 'divine originals' of his imagination.

It was Linnell who, after the completion of the *Job* series, proposed to Blake a series of Dante illustrations. Palmer recalls a visit he paid, with Linnell, on 9 October 1824: 'We found

170 OPPOSITE Illustration to Dante's *Divine Comedy*, 1824–7. *The Inscription over the Gate of Hell.*
171 TOP *Dante Alighieri,* one of a series of heads of poets painted to decorate Hayley's library at Felpham, *c.* 1800–3.
172 ABOVE Illustration to Dante's *Divine Comedy, c.* 1827. *Count Ugolino with his Sons in Prison,* 1827.

King and Priest in his own Household

him lame in bed, of a scalded foot (or leg). There, not inactive, though sixty-seven years old, but hard-working on a bed covered with books sat he up like one of the Antique patriarchs, or a dying Michael Angelo. Thus and there was he making in the leaves of a great book (folio) the sublimest designs for his (not superior) Dante.... He designed them (100 I think) during a fortnight's illness in bed.'

Blake set to work to learn Italian in order to read Dante in the original, using Henry Francis Cary's translation (1805–14)

173 OPPOSITE ABOVE *Divine Comedy, c. 1825–7. Plate 41: The Devils Tormenting Ciampolo.*
174 OPPOSITE BELOW LEFT *Divine Comedy, c. 1825–7. Plate 12: The Devils Mauling Each Other.*
175 OPPOSITE BELOW RIGHT *Divine Comedy, c. 1825–7. Plate 10: Paolo and Francesca.*
176 TOP *Divine Comedy, 1824–7. Lucia Carrying Dante in his Sleep.*
177 ABOVE LEFT *Divine Comedy, 1824–7. The Punishment of Rusticucci and his Companions.*
178 ABOVE RIGHT *Divine Comedy, 1824–7. Dante and Virgil Gazing into the Ditch of Flatterers.*

King and Priest in his own Household

179 OPPOSITE ABOVE *Divine Comedy, 1824–7. The Centaurs and the River of Blood.*
180 OPPOSITE BELOW *Divine Comedy, 1824–7. Dante and Virgil Escaping from the Devils.*
181 TOP *Divine Comedy, 1827. Buoso Donati attacked by the Serpent.*
182 ABOVE *Divine Comedy, 1827. Dante's Foot Striking Bocca degli Abbate.*

King and Priest in his own Household

as a crib. He was a naturally gifted linguist, reading French fairly well, and Latin, Greek and Hebrew a little.

170-83 Like Milton, Dante was, for Blake, a friend and peer in 'great eternity' in whom he nevertheless (as with Milton) found many grave faults. 'Dante saw devils where I saw none,' he told Crabb Robinson. He saw in Dante 'a mere politician and atheist, busied about this world's affairs.... Yet he afterwards spoke 171 of Dante being then with God.' The tempera of Dante's head painted for Hayley's library shows, on one side, a fetter; on the other, a glimpse of Ugolino and his sons in prison – a theme Blake had illustrated in *The Marriage of Heaven and Hell.* The caption reads: 'Does thy God, Oh priest, take such vengeance as this?' Geoffrey Keynes owned another (later) tempera version of this work, in which angels of mercy look down upon the scene of suffering. Milton, Blake criticized for his Puritanical sexual morality; Dante, for his cruelty. Both were worshippers of the moral god, Urizen. His depiction of Hell Gate makes it clear that Blake understood Dante's Hell to be this world, where Satan-Urizen is censed by a worshipping iron-crowned ecclesiastic who kneels before him.

Though thou art worshipped by the names divine
Of Jesus and Jehovah, thou art still
The Son of Morn in weary night's decline
The Lost Traveller's dream under the hill.

It is likely that 'the hill' of these familiar lines is Dante's Mountain of Purgatory, with the hells under it.

Blake's criticisms of Dante are by no means directed against the Catholic faith; on the contrary, the vengeful morality which appalled him in Dante is that of the rational Deism of his own England, against which he waged a lifelong mental fight. Gilchrist reluctantly admitted the admiration Blake in his later years evidently felt, not only for Gothic art, or certain Catholic mystics (especially St Teresa of Avila), but for the Catholic religion:

'If it *must* be told, that he did not go to church, it should also be told that he was no scoffer at sacred mysteries; and, although thus isolated from the communion of the faithful, ever professed his preference of the Church to any sort of sectarianism. On one occasion he expressed the uneasiness he should have felt (had he been a parent) at a child of his dying unbaptized. One day, rather in an opposing mood, I think,

183 *Divine Comedy*, c. 1824–7. The Recording Angel.

he declared that the Romish Church was the only one which taught forgiveness of sins.'

'Forgiveness of sins' was the cornerstone of Christianity, as understood by Blake; this conception is to be found throughout his work from first to last; and it is the central theme of his *Everlasting Gospel*, written in about 1818.

Dante's hells are the states of souls under the tyranny of the unforgiving 'God of this World', 'The Accuser': 'these States Exist now. Man Passes on, but States remain for Ever; he passes thro' them like a traveller who may as well suppose that the places he has passed thro' exist no more, as a Man may suppose that the states he has pass'd thro' Exist no more.' In this, though in no other sense, Hell is eternal.

Albert S. Roe in his commentary on the Dante plates (1953) interprets the work in this sense; as with Milton's works, as with the *Book of Job*, Blake does not merely illustrate, but raises the conception of his original into a new world of meaning.

Dante is the Traveller who explores the 'States'; progressing, as all Mental Travellers must, from the cave or grave of the hells of this world (where spiritual journeys begin) through the circles of purgatory (in which suffering is rendered tolerable by a realization that it is not without use in the purification of souls), to the world of spiritual light. In Blake's terms, he traverses 'the circle of Destiny', which embraces every possible human experience.

184 *The Man sweeping the Interpreter's Parlour*, c. 1822.

185 George Cumberland's visiting card, 1827.

Distinguish therefore States from Individuals in these States.
States change, but Individual Identities never change nor cease,
You cannot go to Eternal Death in that which can never Die.

And Blake adds: 'The imagination is not a State: it is the Human existence itself.'

In about 1824, perhaps stimulated by the gatherings of the Ancients, Blake made a series of watercolours illustrating Bunyan's *Pilgrim's Progress*. Some of these may have been finished by Catherine Blake after his death. His beautiful engraving on pewter, *The Man sweeping the Interpreter's Parlour*, seems to have been completed about the same time from a plate laid aside many years before. In its finished state it is one of the finest and most vigorous of Blake's prints.

184

Blake's *Last Judgment* is his own expression of the 'circle of Destiny'; of the 'States' of the heavens and the hells and the purgatories. The first version of this great theme was painted in 1808 for the Countess of Egremont – a commission obtained for Blake by the miniaturist Ozias Humphry. Blake wrote two descriptions of the picture: one for Ozias Humphry to present to the Countess; another in his Notebook for the year 1810. He had long ago reached a realization beyond the Christian doctrine of an eternity of hell for the damned, and of bliss for the righteous; and indeed he criticized (in *Milton*) Swedenborg himself (whose conception of the Grand Man underlies Blake's vision of the universal collective human kingdom), because he was 'a Samson shorn by the churches', and subscribed to this barbaric doctrine.

He had reached the profounder perspectives of the Indian philosophies, of the Buddhist 'wheel', on which all states are illusory, good and evil alike:

'... I do not consider either the Just or the Wicked to be in a Supreme State, but to be every one of them States of the Sleep which the soul may fall into in its deadly dreams of Good & Evil when it leaves Paradise following the Serpent.'

Blake was working on his final version of *The Last Judgment*, the great fresco (now lost), during the period of his work on Dante. There is no question but that this work was a final attempt to give a complete expression to his vision of the human 'circle of Destiny', in its relation to the 'supreme state' wherein 'Around the Throne Heaven is open'd & Nature of Eternal Things Display'd All Springing from the Divine Humanity.'

During his last months, Blake was 'too much attached to Dante to think much of anything else'. His last completed work was a visiting card for George Cumberland with joyous figures enacting the descent and return of souls, an abridged version of the Arlington Court tempera painting. His young friend Frederick Tatham had commissioned a coloured impression of *The Ancient of Days*, Blake's own singular favourite among all his works. Blake finished it to the utmost point of perfection, making it as beautiful in colour as already grand in design; patiently working on it till within a few days of his death. After he 'had frequently touched upon it, and had frequently held it at a distance, he threw it from him, and with an air of exulting triumph exclaimed, "There! That will do! I cannot mend it."'

As he said these words – so the story continues – 'his glance fell on his loving Kate, no longer young or beautiful, but who had lived with him in these and like humble rooms, in hourly companionship, ever ready helpfulness, and reverent sympathy, for now forty-five years.... "Stay!" he cried, "Keep as you are! *you* have ever been angel to me: I will draw you!" And a portrait was struck off by a hand which approaching death – few days distant now – had not weakened nor benumbed.' The last work to come from Blake's hand was this hasty pencil drawing (now lost) of the faithful companion of his life's hard journey. He died singing his own songs of praise and joy in the vision which illuminated his death, as it had sustained and inspired his life.

Chronology

1757
• Born 28 November at 28 Broad Street, Golden Square, London.

1767
• Sent to Pars' drawing school in the Strand.
• Robert Blake born.

1772
• Began seven-year apprenticeship to James Basire; engraver, Great Queen Street, Lincoln's Inn Fields.

1782
• Married Catherine Boucher 18 August; moved to 23 Green Street, Leicester Fields.

1783
• *Poetical Sketches* published.

1784
• Moved to 27 Broad Street, Golden Square.

1787
• Robert Blake died, February, aged nineteen.
• Moved to 28 Poland Street.

1788
• Plates of *There is No Natural Religion* and of *All Religions are One* etched.

1789
• *Songs of Innocence* and *The Book of Thel* completed.

1790
• *The Marriage of Heaven and Hell* begun.

1791
• Moved to 13 Hercules Buildings, Lambeth.
• The first part of *The French Revolution* printed by Johnson, book-keeper of St Paul's Churchyard; never published.

1793
• Completed *For Children: The Gates of Paradise*; *The Marriage of Heaven and Hell*; *Visions of the Daughters of Albion*; *America: A Prophecy*.

1794
• Completed *Songs of Innocence and of Experience*; *The First Book of Urizen*; *Europe: A Prophecy*.

1795
• Completed *The Song of Los*, *The Book of Ahania*, *The Book of Los*.

1796
• *Vala*, or *The Four Zoas* begun. Designs for Young's *Night Thoughts* begun.

1797
• Engravings for Young's *Night Thoughts* published.

1799
• Introduced by John Flaxman to William Hayley.

1800
• Moved, September, to Felpham, near Bognor, Sussex, under the patronage of Hayley. *Little Tom the Sailor* published.

1802
• Hayley's *Ballads* with Blake's engravings published.

1803
• Quarrel with Trooper Scofield of the Royal Dragoons, in August.
• Returned to London, September, to live at 17 South Molton Street.

1804
• Trial for sedition 11 January at Chichester Assizes. Acquitted.
• The plates for *Milton* and *Jerusalem* begun.

1805
• Blair's *Grave* published with Blake's designs engraved by Schiavonetti.

1808
• *Milton* completed.

1809
• *The Canterbury Pilgrims* exhibited.
• Exhibition of pictures at 28 Broad Street; with *A Descriptive Catalogue*.

1818
• *Jerusalem* completed.
• *For the Sexes: The Gates of Paradise* published.
• Laocoön plate engraved.

1821
• Moved to 3 Fountain Court, Strand.
• Wood engravings for Thornton's *Pastorals of Virgil* completed.

1825
• Engravings for *Illustrations of the Book of Job* published.
• Designs for Dante's *Inferno* begun.

1827
• Seven plates for Dante's *Inferno* engraved.
• Died at Fountain Court, 12 August. Buried in Bunhill Fields.

Select Bibliography

Bentley, G. E. *Blake Records*. New Haven and London: Yale University Press, revised edn, 2004.

Bindman, David. *Blake as an Artist*. Oxford: Phaidon, 1977.

Bindman, David (gen. ed.). *Blake's Illuminated Books*, 6 vols. London: The William Blake Trust and Tate Publishing, 1991–5.

Blunt, Anthony. *The Art of William Blake*. Oxford: Oxford University Press, 1985.

Bronowski, Jacob. *William Blake: A Man Without A Mask*. London: Secker & Warburg, 1943.

Butlin, Martin. *The Paintings and Drawings of William Blake*, 2 vols. New Haven and London: Yale University Press, 1981.

Dent, Shirley and Jason Whittaker. *Radical Blake*. Basingstoke: Palgrave, 2002.

Eaves, Morris. *William Blake's Theory of Art*. Princeton: Princeton University Press, 1981.

Eaves, Morris (ed.). *The Cambridge Companion to William Blake*. Cambridge: Cambridge University Press, 2003.

Erdman, David V. *Blake: Prophet Against Empire*. Princeton: Princeton University Press, 1954.

Erdman, David V. (ed.). *The Complete Poetry and Prose of William Blake*. New York: Anchor Books, 1988.

Ferber, Michael. *The Social Vision of William Blake*. Princeton: Princeton University Press, 1985.

Frye, Northrop. *Fearful Symmetry*. Princeton: Princeton University Press, 1947.

Gilchrist, Alexander. *The Life of William Blake*, 2 vols. London: Macmillan, 1863.

Heppner, Christopher. *Reading Blake's Designs*. Cambridge: Cambridge University Press, 1995.

Mitchell, W. J. T. *Blake's Composite Art*. Princeton: Princeton University Press, 1978.

Myrone, Martin. *The Blake Book*. London: Tate Publishing, 2007.

Raine, Kathleen. *Blake and Tradition*, 2 vols. Cambridge: Cambridge University Press, 1968.

Raine, Kathleen. *Autobiographies* [contains *Farewell Happy Fields*, 1973, *The Land Unknown*, 1975 and *The Lion's Mouth*, 1977]. London: Skoob Books Publishing, 1991.

Townsend, Joyce H. (ed.), *William Blake: The Painter at Work*. London: Tate Publishing, 2003.

Trodd, Colin. *Visions of Blake: William Blake in the Art World, 1830–1930*. Liverpool: Liverpool University Press, 2012.

Viscomi, Joseph. *Blake and the Idea of the Book*. Princeton: Princeton University Press, 1993.

Online Sources

Blake/An Illustrated Quarterly
https://blakequarterly.org/index.php/blake

The Blake Society
http://www.blakesociety.org/

William Blake, Special Issue of *ImageTexT*, 3:2, 2007
http://www.english.ufl.edu/imagetext/archives/v3_2/

The William Blake Archive
http://www.blakearchive.org/

William Blake: The Man from the Future? Special Issue of *Visual Culture in Britain*, 19:3, 2018
www.tandfonline.com doi/full/10.1080/14714787.2018.1533428

List of Illustrations

Dimensions are in centimetres and inches

1785–9. Indian ink, grey wash, 18.1 × 27.3 (7¼ × 10¾). The Fitzwilliam Museum, Cambridge.

27 *Tiriel Supporting the Dying Myratana and Cursing his Sons*, 1786–9. Pen, ink, grey wash, watercolour, 18.7 × 27.3 (7⅜ × 10¾). Yale Center for British Art, New Haven. Paul Mellon Collection.

28 *The Book of Thel*, Plate 2, title-page, 1789. Relief etching, watercolour, 30.5 × 24.1 (12 × 9½). Yale Center for British Art, New Haven. Paul Mellon Collection.

29 *There is No Natural Religion*, Plate 9, *c*. 1788. Relief etching, 13.3 × 10.2 (5¼ × 4). Yale Center for British Art, New Haven. Paul Mellon Collection.

30 *Songs of Innocence*, frontispiece, *c*. 1825. Relief etching, watercolour, gold, 15.7 × 14.1 (6¼ × 5⅝), Metropolitan Museum of Art, New York. Rogers Fund, 1917.

31 *Songs of Innocence and of Experience*, 'The Blossom', *c*. 1825. Relief etching, watercolour, gold, 15.7 × 14.1 (6¼ × 5⅝). Metropolitan Museum of Art, New York. Rogers Fund, 1917.

32 *Songs of Innocence and of Experience*, 'The Ecchoing Green', *c*. 1825. Relief etching, watercolour, gold, 15.7 × 14.1 (6¼ × 5⅝). Metropolitan Museum of Art, New York. Rogers Fund, 1917.

33 *The Book of Thel*, Plate 7, 'Matron Clay', 1789. Relief etching, watercolour, 30.5 × 24.1 (12 × 9½). Yale Center for British Art, New Haven. Paul Mellon Collection.

34 *The Marriage of Heaven and Hell*, 'Nebuchadnezzar', *c*. 1794. Relief etching, hand colouring, colour printing. Library of Congress, Washington, D.C. Rare Book and Special Collections Division. Lessing J. Rosenwald Collection.

35 *The Marriage of Heaven and Hell*, title-page *c*. 1794. Relief etching, hand colouring, colour printing. Library of Congress, Washington, D.C. Rare Book and Special Collections Division. Lessing J. Rosenwald Collection.

36 *The Marriage of Heaven and Hell*, plate 14, 'The soul hovering over the body', *c*. 1796. Relief etching. National Gallery of Art, Washington, D.C. Rosenwald Collection.

37 *For Children: The Gates of Paradise*, Plate 13, 'Aged Ignorance', 1793. Etching, line engraving, 13.7 × 11.4 (5⅜ × 4½). Yale Center for British Art, New Haven. Paul Mellon Collection.

38 *The Marriage of Heaven and Hell*, 'Ugolino and his Sons in Prison', *c*. 1794. Relief and white-line etching, hand colouring, colour printing. Library of Congress, Washington, D.C. Rare Book and Special Collections Division. Lessing J. Rosenwald Collection.

39 *Songs of Innocence and of Experience*, frontispiece, 1794. Relief etching, watercolour,

18.4 × 12.1 (7¼ × 4¾). Yale Center for British Art, New Haven. Paul Mellon Collection.

40 *Songs of Experience*, title-page, *c*. 1825. Relief etching, watercolour, gold, 15.7 × 14.1 (6¼ × 5⅝). Metropolitan Museum of Art, New York. Rogers Fund, 1917.

41 *Songs of Experience*, 'The Sick Rose', *c*. 1825. Relief etching, watercolour, gold, 15.7 × 14.1 (6¼ × 5⅝). Metropolitan Museum of Art, New York. Rogers Fund, 1917.

42 *Songs of Experience*, 'London', *c*. 1825. Relief etching, watercolour, gold, 15.7 × 14.1 (6¼ × 5⅝). Metropolitan Museum of Art, New York. Rogers Fund, 1917.

43 *Songs of Experience*, Plate 42, 'The Tyger', 1794. Relief etching, watercolour, 18.4 × 12.1 (7¼ × 4¾). Yale Center for British Art, New Haven. Paul Mellon Collection.

44 *For Children: The Gates of Paradise*, Plate 4, 'Water', 1793. Etching, line engraving, 13.7 × 11.4 (5⅜ × 4½). Yale Center for British Art, New Haven. Paul Mellon Collection.

45 *For Children: The Gates of Paradise*, Plate 5, 'Earth', 1793. Etching, line engraving, 13.7 × 11.4 (5⅜ × 4½). Yale Center for British Art, New Haven. Paul Mellon Collection.

46 *For Children: The Gates of Paradise*, Plate 18, 'I have said to the Worm....', 1793. Etching, line engraving, 13.7 × 11.4 cm (5⅜ × 4½). Yale Center for British Art, New Haven. Paul Mellon Collection.

47 *For Children: The Gates of Paradise*, Plate 6, 'Air', 1793. Etching, line engraving, 13.7 × 11.4 (5⅜ × 4½). Yale Center for British Art, New Haven. Paul Mellon Collection.

48 *For Children: The Gates of Paradise*, Plate 7, 'Fire', 1793. Etching, line engraving, 13.7 × 11.4 cm (5⅜ × 4½). Yale Center for British Art, New Haven. Paul Mellon Collection.

49 *Visions of the Daughters of Albion*, frontispiece, 1793. Relief etching, watercolour, 17.1 × 11.7 (6¾ × 4⅝). Yale Center for British Art, New Haven. Paul Mellon Collection.

50 *Visions of the Daughters of Albion*, title-page, 1793. Relief etching, watercolour, 16.5 × 12.7 (6½ × 5). Yale Center for British Art, New Haven. Paul Mellon Collection

51 *America: A Prophecy*, Plate 12, 'Thus Wept the Angel Voice....', 1793. Relief etching, watercolour, 36.8 × 26.7 (14½ × 10½). Yale Center for British Art, New Haven. Paul Mellon Collection.

52 *America: A Prophecy*, title-page, 1793. Relief etching, watercolour, 36.8 × 26.7 (14½ × 10½). Yale Center for British Art, New Haven. Paul Mellon Collection.

53 *America: A Prophecy*, frontispiece, 1973.

Relief etching, watercolour, 36.8 × 26.7
(14½ × 10½). Yale Center for British Art,
New Haven. Paul Mellon Collection.
54 *America: A Prophecy*, Plate 3, 'Preludium/
The shadowy daughter....,' 1793. Relief etching,
watercolour, 36.8 × 26.7 (14½ × 10½). Yale
Center for British Art, New Haven. Paul Mellon
Collection.
55 *America: A Prophecy*, Plate 4, 'Silent
as despairing love...', 1793. Relief etching,
watercolour, 36.8 × 26.7 (14½ × 10½). Yale
Center for British Art, New Haven. Paul Mellon
Collection.
56 *America: A Prophecy*, cancelled plate,
'A Dream of Thiralatha', *c.* 1794–6. Relief etching,
11.8 × 17.2 (4⅝ × 6¾). National Gallery
of Art, Washington, D.C. Rosenwald Collection.
57 *Europe: A Prophecy*, Plate 10, 'Enitharmon
slept....', 1794. Relief etching, pen, ink, oil,
watercolour, 37.5 × 26.7 (14¾ × 10½). Yale
Center for British Art, New Haven. Paul Mellon
Collection.
58 *Europe: A Prophecy*, Plate 14, 'And the
clouds & fires....', 1794. Relief etching, pen, ink,
oil, watercolour, 37.5 × 26.7 (14¾ × 10½). Yale
Center for British Art, New Haven. Paul Mellon
Collection.
59 *Europe: A Prophecy*, Plate 7, 'Now comes
the night....', 1794. Relief etching, pen, ink, oil,
watercolour, 37.5 × 26.7 (14¾ × 10½). Yale Center
for British Art, New Haven. Paul Mellon Collection.
60 *Europe: A Prophecy*, Plate 12, 'Albions
Angel rose....', 1794. Relief etching, pen, ink,
oil, watercolour, 37.5 × 26.7 (14¾ × 10½). Yale
Center for British Art, New Haven. Paul Mellon
Collection.
61 *Europe: A Prophecy*, frontispiece, 1794.
Relief etching, pen, ink, oil, watercolour, 37.5 ×
26.7 (14¾ × 10½). Yale Center for British Art, New
Haven. Paul Mellon Collection.
62 *The First Book of Urizen*, Plate 7, 'As the stars
are apart from the earth....', 1794. Relief etching,
watercolour, 30.2 × 24.4 (11⅞ × 9⅝). Yale Center
for British Art, New Haven, Paul Mellon Collection.
63 *The First Book of Urizen*, Plate 21, 1794.
Relief etching, watercolour, 30.2 × 24.4
(11⅞ × 9⅝). Yale Center for British Art, New
Haven. Paul Mellon Collection.
64 *The First Book of Urizen*, Plate 18, 1794. Relief
etching, hand colouring, 11.9 × 10.5 (4¾ × 4¼).
The British Museum, London.
65 *The First Book of Urizen*, Plate 16, 1794.
Relief etching, watercolour, 30.2 × 24.4
(11⅞ × 9⅝). Yale Center for British Art,
New Haven. Paul Mellon Collection.

66 *The First Book of Urizen*, Plate 5, 1794.
Relief etching, watercolour, 30.2 × 24.4
(11⅞ × 9⅝). Yale Center for British Art,
New Haven. Paul Mellon Collection.
67 Page from *The Four Zoas*, or *Vala*, 1797.
Pen, ink, pencil, crayon, charcoal, 41.4 × 32.8
(16⅜ × 13). British Library, London.
68 *The Death of the Wife of the Biblical Prophet
Ezekiel*, *c.* 1785, Pen, ink, wash over graphite,
34.6 × 47.9 (13⅝ × 18⅞). Philadelphia Museum.
Gift of Mrs William Thomas Tonner, 1964
69 *Elohim Creating Adam*, 1795–*c.* 1805.
Colour print, ink, watercolour, 43.1 × 53.6
(17 × 21⅛). Tate, London. Photo Tate London.
70 *Newton*, 1795–*c*.1805. Colour print, ink,
watercolour, 46 × 60 (18⅛ × 23⅝). Tate, London.
Photo Tate London.
71 *Nebuchadnezzar*, 1795. 43 × 60.3 (17 × 23¾).
Colour monotype, tempera, pen, ink,
watercolour. Minneapolis Institute of Art. The
Miscellaneous Works of Art Purchase Fund, 1957.
72 *The Night of Enitharmon's Joy* (formerly called
Hecate), *c.* 1795. Colour print, ink, tempera,
watercolour, 43.9 × 58.1 (17⅜ × 22⅞). Tate,
London. Photo Tate London.
73 *The House of Death*, 1795–*c.* 1805. Colour print,
ink, watercolour, 48.5 × 61 (19⅛ × 24⅛). Tate,
London. Photo Tate London.
74 *Satan Exulting over Eve*, *c.* 1795. Colour print,
graphite, pen, ink, watercolour, 42.5 × 53.5 (16¾ ×
21⅛). The J. Paul Getty Museum, Los Angeles.
75 *Pity*, *c.* 1795. Colour print, ink, watercolour,
42.5 × 53.9 (16¾ × 21¼). Tate, London. Photo Tate
London.
76 *God Judging Adam*, *c.* 1795. Relief etching,
pen, ink, watercolour, 42.5 × 52.7 (16¾ × 20¾).
Metropolitan Museum of Art, New York. Rogers
Fund, 1916.
77 *The Good and Evil Angels*, 1795–*c.* 1805.
Colour print, ink, watercolour, 44.5 × 59.4
(17⅝ × 23½). Tate, London. Photo Tate London.
78 *The Marriage of Heaven and Hell*, *c.* 1794.
Relief etching, hand colouring, colour printing.
Library of Congress, Washington, D.C. Rare
Book and Special Collections Division. Lessing J.
Rosenwald Collection.
79 *Joseph of Arimathea Preaching to the Britons*,
c. 1794–6. Relief etching, pen, watercolour,
32.1 × 24.1 (12⅝ × 9½). National Gallery of Art,
Washington, D.C. Rosenwald Collection.
80 Vitruvian Man, from Cornelius Agrippa's
Three Books of Occult Philosophy, page 268, 1651.
81 Drawing, *c.* 1780. Pencil, 20.5 × 28.5
(8⅛ × 11¼). Victoria and Albert Museum, London.
Photo Victoria and Albert Museum, London.

82 *Glad Day (The Dance of Albion)* from *A Large Book of Designs*, 1794–6. Engraving, etching, hand colouring, 27.2 × 20 (10¾ × 7⅞). The British Museum, London.

83 Page from *The Four Zoas*, or *Vala*, 1797. Pen, ink, pencil, crayon, charcoal, 40.9 x 31.9 (16⅛ x 12⅝). British Library, London.

84 Page from *The Four Zoas*, or *Vala*, 1797. Pen, ink, pencil, watercolour, crayon, charcoal, 41.3 x 31.3 (16⅜ x 12⅜). British Library, London.

85 Page from *The Four Zoas*, or *Vala*, 1797. Pen, ink, pencil, crayon, charcoal, 40.8 x 32.4 (16⅛ x 12⅞). British Library, London.

86 Page from *The Four Zoas*, or *Vala*, 1797. Pen, ink, pencil, crayon, charcoal, 39.4 x 32.3 (15⅝ x 12¾). British Library, London.

87 Page from *The Four Zoas*, or *Vala*, 1797. Pen, ink, pencil, crayon, charcoal, 41.2 x 32.4 (16¼ x 12⅞). British Library, London.

88 *The Poems of Thomas Gray*, Design 57, 'The Bard: A Pindaric Ode', 1797–8. Watercolour, pen, ink, graphite, 41.9 x 32.4 (16½ x 12¾). Yale Center for British Art, New Haven. Paul Mellon Collection.

89 *The Poems of Thomas Gray*, Design 9, 'Ode on the Death of a Favourite Cat', 1797–8. Watercolour, pen, ink, graphite, 41.9 × 32.4 (16½ × 12¾). Yale Center for British Art, New Haven. Paul Mellon Collection.

90 *The Poems of Thomas Gray*, Design 7, 'Ode on the Death of a Favourite Cat', 1797–8. Watercolour, pen, ink, graphite, 41.9 × 32.4 (16½ × 12¾). Yale Center for British Art, New Haven. Paul Mellon Collection.

91 *The Poems of Thomas Gray*, Design 15, 'Ode on a Distant Prospect of Eton College', 1797–8. Watercolour, pen, ink, graphite, 41.9 x 32.4 (16½ x 12¾). Yale Center for British Art, New Haven. Paul Mellon Collection.

92 *The Poems of Thomas Gray, Design 17*, 'Ode on a Distant Prospect of Eton College', 1797–8. Watercolour, pen, ink, graphite, 41.9 x 32.4 (16½ x 12¾). Yale Center for British Art, New Haven. Paul Mellon Collection.

93 *The Poems of Thomas Gray*, 'Ode on a Distant Prospect of Eton College', 1797–8. Watercolour, pen, ink, graphite, 41.9 x 32.4 (16½ x 12¾). Yale Center for British Art, New Haven. Paul Mellon Collection.

94 Young's *Night Thoughts*, title-page, 'Night the First: On Life, Death and Immortality', *c.* 1797. Etching, engraving, watercolour, 41.9 × 32.1 (16½ × 12⅝). Yale Center for British Art, New Haven. Paul Mellon Collection.

95 Young's *Night Thoughts*, Page 65, 'Night the Fourth, The Christian Triumph', *c.* 1797. Etching, engraving, watercolour, 41.9 × 32.1 (16½ × 12⅝).

Yale Center for British Art, New Haven. Paul Mellon Collection.

96 Young's *Night Thoughts*, page 46, 'Where sense runs savage broke from reason's chain', *c.* 1797. Etching, engraving, watercolour, 41.9 × 32.1 (16½ × 12⅝). Yale Center for British Art, New Haven. Paul Mellon Collection.

97 *The Body of Christ Borne to the Tomb, c.* 1799–1800. Tempera, 26.7 × 37.8 (10⅝ × 15). Tate, London. Photo Tate London.

98 *Job and his Daughters*, 1799–1800. Pen, tempera, 27.3 × 38.4 (10¾ × 15⅛). National Gallery of Art, Washington, D.C. Rosenwald Collection.

99 *The Angel Appearing to Zacharias*, 1799–1800. Pen, ink, tempera, 26.7 × 38.1 (10½ × 15). Metropolitan Museum of Art, New York. Bequest of William Church Osborn, 1951.

100 *Christ Giving Sight to Bartimaeus*, 1799–1800. Pen, ink, tempera, 26 × 38.1 (10¼ × 15). Yale Center for British Art, New Haven. Paul Mellon Collection.

101 *Mary Magdalene Washing Christ's Feet*, *c.* 1805. Pen, ink, watercolour, 34.9 × 34.6 (13¾ × 13⅝). Philadelphia Museum of Art. Gift of Mrs William Thomas Tonner, 1964.

102 *Mary Magdalene at the Sepulchre, c.* 1805. Pen, ink, watercolour, 43.8 × 31.1 (17¼ × 12¼). Yale Center for British Art, New Haven. Paul Mellon Collection.

103 *Jephthah Met by his Daughter, c.* 1803. Pen, ink, watercolour, 36.2 × 41.6 (14¼ × 16⅜). Philadelphia Museum of Art. Gift of Mrs William Thomas Tonner, 1964.

104 *The Soldiers Casting Lots for Christ's Garments*, 1800. 42 × 31.4 (16⅝ × 12⅜). Pen, ink, grey wash, watercolour. Fitzwilliam Museum, Cambridge. Photo Fitzwilliam Museum, University of Cambridge/Bridgeman Images.

105 *Songs of Experience*, 'To Tirzah', *c.* 1825. Relief etching, watercolour, gold, 15.7 × 14.1 (6¼ × 5 5/8). Metropolitan Museum of Art, New York. Rogers Fund, 1917.

106 *Jerusalem*, Plate 25, 'And there was heard....', 1804–20. Relief etching, pen, ink, watercolour, gold, 34.3 × 26.4 (13½ × 10⅜). Yale Center for British Art, New Haven. Paul Mellon Collection.

107 From Milton's *Paradise Lost*, Illustration 2, 'Satan, Sin and Death: Satan Comes to the Gates of Hell'. 1807. 24.7 × 20.8 (9¾ × 8¼). Ink, watercolour. The Huntington Library, Art Collections and Botanical Gardens, San Marino. Photo courtesy of the Huntington Art Collections, San Marino.

108 *The Lord Answering Job from the Whirlwind, c.* 1799. Pen, ink, pencil, watercolour, 39.3 × 33 (15½ × 13). National Galleries of Scotland. Presented by the trustees of Mr Graham

Robertson 1949 through the Art Fund.

109 *David Delivered out of Many Waters*, *c.* 1805. Ink, watercolour, 41.5 × 34.8 (16⅜ × 13¾). Tate, London. Photo Tate London.

110 *The Whirlwind: Ezekiel's Vision of the Cherubim and Eyed Wheels*, *c.* 1803–5. Pen, watercolour, 39.4 × 29.5 (15½ × 11⅝). Museum of Fine Arts, Boston. Museum purchase with funds donated by contribution 90.108. Photo Museum of Fine Arts, Boston.

111 *Famine*, 1805. Watercolour, pencil, 29.5 × 38.9 (11⅝ × 15⅜). Museum of Fine Arts, Boston. Museum purchase with funds donated by contribution 90.104. Photo Museum of Fine Arts, Boston.

112 *The Body of Abel found by Adam and Eve*, *c.* 1826. Ink, tempera, gold, 32.5 × 43.3 (12⅞ × 17⅛). Tate, London. Photo Tate London.

113 *The Nativity*, *c.* 1799–1800. Tempera, 27.3 × 38.3 (10¾ × 15⅛). Philadelphia Museum of Art. Gift of Mrs William Thomas Tonner, 1964-110-1.

114 *The Agony in the Garden*, *c.* 1799–1800. Tempera, 27 × 38 (10¾ × 15). Tate, London. Photo Tate London.

115 *The Parable of the Wise and Foolish Virgins*, *c.* 1799–1800. Watercolour, pen, ink, 36 × 32.2 (14¼ × 12¾). Metropolitan Museum of Art, New York. Rogers Fund, 1914.

116 *The Angel Michael Binding Satan* (*He Cast him into the Bottomless Pit, and Shut him up*), *c.* 1805. Watercolour, ink, graphite, 35.9 × 32.5 (14¼ × 12⅞). Harvard Art Museums/Fogg Museum. Gift of W. A. White, 1915.8. Photo Imaging Department/President and Fellows of Harvard College.

117 *The River of Life*, c.1805. Ink, watercolour, 30.5 × 33.6 (12⅛ × 13¼). Tate, London. Photo Tate London.

118 *Last Judgment*, 1808. Watercolour, 50.3 × 40 (19⅞ × 15¾). Petworth House, Sussex. Photo Petworth House, Sussex/National Trust Photographic Library/John Hammond/ Bridgeman Images.

119 *Jacob's Ladder*, *c.* 1799–1806. Watercolour, pen, 39.8 × 30.6 (15¾ × 12⅛). The British Museum, London.

120 *Angel of the Divine Presence Bringing Eve to Adam*, *c.* 1803. Watercolour, pen, ink, 41.6 × 33.2 (16½ × 12¾). Metropolitan Museum of Art, New York. Rogers Fund, 1906.

121 From Milton's *Paradise Lost*, 'The Archangel Raphael with Adam and Eve', 1808. Pen, watercolour, 49.8 × 39.8 (19⅝ × 15¾). Museum of Fine Arts, Boston. Museum purchase with funds donated by contribution. 90.97. Photo Museum of Fine Arts, Boston.

122 *The Last Supper*, 1799. Tempera, 30.5 × 48.3 (12 × 19). National Gallery of Art, Washington, D.C.

123 From William Hayley's *Ballads*, 'The Horse', 1805. Engraving, 10.8 × 7.3 (4¼ × 2⅞). Connecticut College. The Wetmore Print Collection.

124 From William Hayley's *Ballads*, 'The Dog', 1805. Engraving, 16.5 × 14 (6½ × 5½). Connecticut College. The Wetmore Print Collection.

125 From William Hayley's *Ballads*, 'The Eagle', 1805. Engraving, 14 × 9.85 (5⅝ × 4). Connecticut College. The Wetmore Print Collection.

126 From *Milton: A Poem*, 'When on the highest lift....', *c.* 1804–8. Etching. New York Public Library.

127 *Songs of Experience*, 'The Little Girl Found', 1789. Relief etching, pen, ink, watercolour, 18.4 × 12.1 (7¼ × 4 ¾). Yale Center for British Art, New Haven. Paul Mellon Collection.

128 Illustration to William Cowper's poem, 'The Task', *Winter*, *c.* 1820–5. Tempera, 90.2 × 29.7 (35⅝ × 11¾). Tate, London. Photo Tate London.

129 Illustration to William Cowper's poem, 'The Task', *Evening*, *c.* 1820–5. Watercolour, chalk, 91.8 × 29.7 (36¼ × 11¾). National Gallery of Art, Washington, D.C.

130 From *Milton: A Poem*, Plate 18, 'To Annihilate the Falsehood of Self-Deceit and False Forgiveness', *c.* 1804–8. Etching. New York Public Library.

131 From Milton's *Paradise Lost*, 'The Temptation and Fall of Eve', 1808. Pen, watercolour, 49.7 × 38.7 (19⅝ × 15¼). Museum of Fine Arts, Boston. Museum purchase with funds donated by contribution. 90.99. Photo Museum of Fine Arts, Boston.

132 From Milton's *Paradise Lost*, 'Satan Watching the Caresses of Adam and Eve', 1808. Pen, watercolour, 50.5 × 38 (20 × 15). Museum of Fine Arts, Boston. Museum purchase with funds donated by contribution. 90.96. Photo Museum of Fine Arts, Boston.

133 *Christ Tempted by Satan to Turn the Stones to Bread*, *c.* 1816–18. Pen, ink, grey wash, watercolour, 16.8 × 13.3 (6⅝ × 5¼). Fitzwilliam Museum, University of Cambridge. Photo Fitzwilliam Museum, University of Cambridge/ Bridgeman Images.

134 From Milton's *Comus*, Illustration 5, 'The Magic Banquet with the Lady Spell-Bound', *c.* 1801. Pen, watercolour, 22.1 × 17.9 (8¾ × 7⅛). The Huntington Library, Art Collections, and Botanical Gardens, San Marino. Photo courtesy of the Huntington Art Collections, San Marino.

135 From Milton's *Comus*, Illustration 1, 'Comus and his Levellers', *c.* 1801. Pen, watercolour, 21.6 × 18.1 (8⅝ × 7¼). The Huntington Library, Art Collections, and Botanical Gardens, San

Marino. Photo courtesy of the Huntington Art Collections, San Marino.

136 From Milton's *Hymn on the Morning of Christ's Nativity*, Illustration 2, 'The Annunciation to the Shepherds', *c.* 1814–6. Pen, watercolour, 15.9 × 12.6 (6⅜ × 5). The Huntington Library, Art Collections, and Botanical Gardens, San Marino. Photo courtesy of the Huntington Art Collections, San Marino.

137 From Milton's *Hymn on the Morning of Christ's Nativity*, Illustration 1, 'The Descent of Peace', *c.* 1814–16. Pen, watercolour, 15.9 × 12.6 (6⅜ × 5). The Huntington Library, Art Collections, and Botanical Gardens, San Marino. Photo courtesy of the Huntington Art Collections, San Marino.

138 From *Paradise Regained*, 'Christ's troubled sleep', *c.* 1816–18. Watercolour, 16.8 × 13.3 (6⅝ × 5¼). Fitzwilliam Museum, University of Cambridge. Photo Fitzwilliam Museum, University of Cambridge/Bridgeman Images.

139 *Jerusalem*, title-page, 1804–20. Relief etching, watercolour, gold, pen, ink, 34.3 × 26.4 (13½ × 10⅜). Yale Center for British Art, New Haven. Paul Mellon Collection.

140 *Jerusalem*, Plate 18, 'From every-one of the Four Regions....', 1804–20. Relief etching, watercolour, pen, ink, 34.3 × 26.4 (13½ × 10⅜). Yale Center for British Art, New Haven. Paul Mellon Collection.

141 *Jerusalem*, Plate 53, 1804–20. Relief etching, watercolour, gold, pen, ink, 34.3 × 26.4 (13½ × 10⅜). Yale Center for British Art, New Haven. Paul Mellon Collection

142 *Jerusalem*, Plate 28, proof impression, *c.* 1820. Relief etching, watercolour, pen, ink, 11.1 × 15.9 (4⅜ × 6¼). Yale Center for British Art, New Haven. Paul Mellon Collection.

143 *Jerusalem*, Plate 62, 'Repose on me....', 1804–20. Relief etching, watercolour, pen, ink, 34.3 × 26.4 (13½ × 10⅜). Yale Center for British Art, New Haven. Paul Mellon Collection.

144 *Jerusalem*, Plate 97, 'Awake! Awake Jerusalem....', 1804–20. Relief etching, watercolour, gold, pen, ink, 34.3 × 26.4 (13½ × 10⅜). Yale Center for British Art, New Haven. Paul Mellon Collection.

145 *Jerusalem*, Plate 32, 'Leaning against the pillars....', 1804–20. Relief etching, watercolour, pen, ink, 34.3 × 26.4 (13½ × 10⅜). Yale Center for British Art, New Haven. Paul Mellon Collection.

146 *Jerusalem*, Plate 99, 'All Human Forms identified....', 1804–20. Relief etching, watercolour, pen, ink, 34.3 × 26.4 (13½ × 10⅜). Yale Center for British Art, New Haven. Paul Mellon Collection.

147 *Jerusalem*, Plate 76, 1804–20. Relief etching, watercolour, gold, pen, ink, 34.3 × 26.4 (13½ × 10⅜). Yale Center for British Art, New Haven.

Paul Mellon Collection.

148 *Jerusalem*, Plate 39, 'By Satans Watch-friends....', 1804–20. Relief etching, watercolour, gold, pen, ink, 34.3 × 26.4 (13½ × 10⅜). Yale Center for British Art, New Haven. Paul Mellon Collection.

149 From Robert Blair's *The Grave*, 'The Counsellor, King, Warrior, Mother and Child in the Tomb', 1808, published 1813. Etching, 28.9 × 38.1 (11⅜ × 15). Yale Center for British Art, New Haven. Paul Mellon Collection.

150 Chaucer's *Canterbury Pilgrims*, 1810–20. Engraving, 34.9 × 95.6 (13¾ × 37⅝). Yale Center for British Art, New Haven. Paul Mellon Collection.

151 *The Spiritual Form of Nelson Guiding Leviathan*, *c.* 1805–9. Tempera, 76.2 × 62.5 (30 × 24⅝). Tate, London. Photo Tate London.

152 Copy of the *Laocoön*, for Rees's *Cyclopædia*, 1815. Graphite, 32.1 × 22.9 (12⅝ × 9). Yale Center for British Art, New Haven. Paul Mellon Fund.

153 John Linnell, *Portrait of William Blake*, 1820. Pencil, 20.1 × 15.5 (8 × 6⅛). Fitzwilliam Museum, University of Cambridge.

154 Attributed to John Linnell, *The Man Who Taught Blake Painting in his Dreams* (after William Blake), *c.* 1825. 26 × 20.6 (10¼ × 8⅛). Tate, London. Photo Tate London.

155 *The Head of a Ghost of a Flea*, *c.* 1819. Graphite, 18.9 × 15.3 (7½ × 6⅛). Tate, London. Photo Tate London.

156 *The Ghost of a Flea*, *c.* 1819–20. Tempera, gold, 21.4 × 16.2 (8½ × 6½). Tate, London. Photo Tate London.

157 From Thornton's *Pastorals of Virgil*, 'Thenot Remonstrates with Colinet', 1821. Engraving, 3.8 × 7.3 (1½ × 2⅞). Metropolitan Museum of Art, New York. Harris Brisbane Dick Fund, 1932.

158 From Thornton's *Pastorals of Virgil*, 'Colinet departs in sorrow', 1820–1. Engraving, 3.5 × 7.5 (1½ × 3). Rijksmuseum, Amsterdam

159 From Thornton's *Pastorals of Virgil*, 'Blasted Trees and Flattened Crops', 1821. Engraving, 3.5 × 7.3 (1⅜ × 2⅞). Metropolitan Museum of Art, New York. Harris Brisbane Dick Fund, 1932.

160 Drawing for Thornton's *Virgil*, 1820. 'Thenot'.

161 *Job in Prosperity*, Plate 1, 1825. Engraving, 50.5 × 34.3 (19⅞ × 13½). Los Angeles County Museum of Art. Gift of Miss Bella Mabury for the Paul Rodman Mabury Collection.

162 *The Wrath of Elihu*, Plate 12, 1825–6. Engraving, 41.3 × 27.6 (16 1/4 × 10⅞). The Metropolitan Museum of Art, New York. Gift of Edward Bement, 1917.

163 from *The Book of Job*, Plate 15, 'God Pointing out Behemoth... and Leviathan', 1825. Engraving, 55.9 × 45.6 (22 × 18). Los Angeles County Museum of Art. Gift of Miss Bella Mabury for the Paul

Rodman Mabury Collection.

164 From *The Book of Job*, Plate 20, 'Job Recounting his Experiences to his Daughters', 1825. Engraving, 50.8 × 34.3 (20 × 13½). Los Angeles County Museum of Art. Gift of Miss Bella Mabury for the Paul Rodman Mabury Collection.

165 *Satan Smiting Job with Sore Boils, c.* 1826. Ink, tempera, 32.6 × 43.2 (12⅞ × 17⅛). Tate, London. Photo Tate London.

166 From *The Book of Job*, Plate 3, 'Satan Bringing Destruction on the Sons and Daughters of Job', 1825. Engraving, 50.5 × 34.3 (19⅞ × 13½). Los Angeles County Museum of Art. Gift of Miss Bella Mabury for the Paul Rodman Mabury Collection.

167 From *The Book of Job*, Plate 6, 'Satan Smiting Job with Sore Boils', 1825. Engraving. National Gallery of Art, Washington, D.C. Rosenwald Collection.

168 From *The Book of Job*, Plate 13, 'God Appearing in the Whirlwind', 1825. Engraving, 50.5 × 34.3 (19⅞ ×13½). Los Angeles County Museum of Art. Gift of Miss Bella Mabury for the Paul Rodman Mabury Collection.

169 *The Sea of Time and Place*, 1821. Pen, ink, watercolour, 40 × 49.5 (15¾ × 19½). Arlington Court, Devon. Photo Arlington Court, Devon/ National Trust Photographic Library/John Hammond/Bridgeman Images.

170 Illustration to Dante's *Divine Comedy*, 'The Inscription over the Gate of Hell', 1824–7. Graphite, ink, watercolour, 52.7 × 37.4 (20¾ × 14¾). Tate, London. Photo Tate London.

171 *Dante Alighieri, c.*1800–3. Pen, ink, tempera, 42.5 × 87.8 (16¾ × 34⅝). Manchester Art Gallery. Photo Manchester Art Gallery/Bridgeman Images.

172 From Dante's *Divine Comedy*, 'Count Ugolino and his Sons in Prison', *c.* 1827. Tempera, 33 × 44 (13 × 17¾). Fitzwilliam Museum, Cambridge. Photo Fitzwilliam Museum, University of Cambridge/Bridgeman Images.

173 From Dante's *Inferno*, Plate 41, 'The Circle of Corrupt Officials: The Devils Tormenting Ciampolo', *c.* 1825–7. Engraving, 23.8 × 33.7 (9⅜ × 13¼). Metropolitan Museum of Art, New York. Rogers Fund, 1917.

174 From Dante's *Inferno*, Plate 12, 'The Circle of Corrupt Officials: The Devils Mauling Each Other', *c.* 1825–7. Engraving, 23.8 × 33.7 (9⅜ × 13¼). Metropolitan Museum of Art, New York. Rogers Fund, 1917.

175 From Dante's *Inferno*, Plate 10, 'The Circle of the Lustful: Paolo and Francesca', *c.*1825–7. Engraving, 23.8 × 33.7 (9⅜ × 13¼). Metropolitan Museum of Art, New York. Rogers Fund, 1917.

176 From Dante's *Divine Comedy*, 'Lucia Carrying Dante in his Sleep', 1824–7. Watercolour, graphite, ink, chalk, 37.2 × 52.2 (14⅝ × 20½). Harvard Art Museums/Fogg Museum. Bequest of Grenville L. Winthrop, 1943.438. Photo Imaging Department/ President and Fellows of Harvard College.

177 From Dante's *Divine Comedy*, 'The Punishment of Rusticucci and His Companions', 1824–7. Watercolour, ink, graphite, chalk, 37 × 52.3 (14⅝ × 20⅝). Harvard Art Museums/Fogg Museum. Bequest of Grenville L. Winthrop, 1943.447. Photo Imaging Department/President and Fellows of Harvard College.

178 From Dante's *Divine Comedy*, 'Dante and Virgil Gazing into the Ditch of Flatterers', 1824–7. Watercolour, ink, graphite, chalk, 37 × 52.3 (14⅝ × 20⅝). Harvard Art Museums/Fogg Museum. Bequest of Grenville L. Winthrop, 1943.435. Photo Imaging Department/President and Fellows of Harvard College.

179 From Dante's *Divine Comedy*, 'The Centaurs and the River of Blood', 1824–7. Watercolour, ink, graphite, chalk, 37.1 × 32.3 (14⅝ × 12¾). Harvard Art Museums/Fogg Museum. Bequest of Grenville L. Winthrop, 1943.444. Photo Imaging Department/President and Fellows of Harvard College.

180 From Dante's *Divine Comedy*, 'Dante and Virgil Escaping from the Devils', 1824–7. Watercolour, ink, graphite, chalk, 52.3 × 36.9 (20⅝ × 14⅝). Harvard Art Museums/Fogg Museum. Bequest of Grenville L. Winthrop, 1943.443. Photo Imaging Department/President and Fellows of Harvard College.

181 From *Dante's Inferno*, 'The Circle of the Thieves: Buoso Donati Attacked by the Serpent', 1827. Engraving, 23.9 × 33.6 (9½ × 13¼). The Art Institute of Chicago. Gift of Mrs Elizabeth D. McCormick.

182 From Dante's *Inferno*, 'The Circle of the Traitors: Dante's Foot Striking Bocca degli Abbate', 1827. Engraving, 23.4 × 33.9 cm (9¼ × 13⅜ in.). The Art Institute of Chicago. Gift of Mrs Elizabeth D. McCormick.

183 From Dante's *Divine Comedy*, 'The Recording Angel', *c.* 1824–7. Pen, ink, pencil, watercolour, 52 × 36 cm (20½ × 14¼ in.). Birmingham Museums and Art Gallery. Photo Birmingham Museums and Art Gallery.

184 *The Man Sweeping the Interpreter's Parlour, c.* 1822. Engraving, 17.8 × 23.2 cm (7⅛ × 9¼ in.). Yale Center for British Art, New Haven. Paul Mellon Collection.

185 *George Cumberland's Message Card*, 1827. Engraving, 3.3 × 8.3 cm (1⅜ × 3⅜ in.). Metropolitan Museum of Art, New York. Gift of William E. Baillie, 1925.

Index

The World of Art series is a comprehensive,
accessible, indispensable companion to the history
of art and its latest developments, covering themes,
artists and movements that span centuries and
the gamut of visual culture around the globe.

You may also like:

**Five Centuries of British
Painting**
Andrew Wilton

Gainsborough
William Vaughan

Monet
James H. Rubin

Turner
Graham Reynolds
Introduction by
David Blayney Brown

World of Art

For more information about
Thames & Hudson, and the World of Art
series, visit **thamesandhudsonusa.com**